Restoring a Dream

My Journey Restoring a 1960 Airstream

Tim Shephard

First Printing: January 2013

ISBN-13: 978-1480280571
ISBN-10: 1480280577

Edited by: Dave McCrostie
Cover photo by: Debra Shephard/The Grand Tetons National Park

Website: www.restoringadream.com

Disclaimer

This book and the Vintage Airstream Podcast are for entertainment purposes only. Our opinions are not instructions, but simply our own personal experiences expressed in word or print. As such we are not responsible for any damage to property or personal injury.

the VAP and the author makes no warranties, expressed or implied, as to the completeness, accuracy, or practicality of such procedure or any information contained in this book. Be sure to always exercise reasonable caution, follow applicable codes and regulations, and consult with a professional if in doubt about any procedures.

From the creator of The Vintage Airstream Podcast

The Vintage Airstream Podcast, also known as theVAP, is an Internet radio program for Airstream enthusiasts. Listeners can subscribe to the show using an application such as iTunes, or they can download the episodes directly from theVAP.com. Tim Shephard created the program in August of 2005.

The purpose of the show is to aid vintage Airstream owners by answering their questions on restoration topics. The concept of the show is similar to a 'car talk' program where listeners call in with their questions. The program host, Tim Shephard, and a Panel of Pros answer these questions. Colin Hyde and Rob Baker were the show's first Panel Pros. Over the years they've answered questions covering almost every aspect of vintage Airstream restoration.

Colin Hyde: As the owner of Colin Hyde Trailer Restorations, Colin has an extensive background in the service and repair of vintage Airstreams. Colin Hyde is widely respected as an expert in Airstream trailer restorations. He can be found on the web at: www.colinhydetrailerrestorations.com.

Rob Baker: Rob is an Airstream enthusiast who has owned 23 vintage Airstreams. Originally Rob owned a 1985 Airstream 34' Limited but gave it up to 'go vintage'. Rob now has a 1958 Sovereign of the Road that underwent an extensive ground up restoration. He has helped many newbies become Airstream owners and has shared his knowledge and experiences on theVAP as a panel pro for five years. Rob can be found at: www.sweetsovereign.blogspot.com.

Author

Tim Shephard, creator and host of the Vintage Airstream Podcast, has restored and traveled across the United States in his 1960 Airstream Ambassador. Tim and his wife, Debra, live in Northern California with their family and have enjoyed traveling in their Airstreams for the past 10 years. Their longest trip so far was from California to Florida when they were on the road for 30 nights.

In the photo above, Tim is leaning on a piece of a meteor that formed a 550-foot deep crater in Arizona.

Dedications

First to my wife, Debra and our children, who had to be quiet every
other Thursday from 7 to 9pm.

~

To all the listeners and fans of the Vintage Airstream Podcast.

~

To Colin, Rob, and Frank, the real Pros.

~

Finally to my dad who helped me recover my Ambassador.
Dad has listened to every episode since the beginning, even though he
has never owned a trailer.

Acknowledgements

I'd like to thank my wife, Debra, who puts up with my aluminum obsession, including two trailer restorations, and over 7 years of recording the VAP. Debra took the cover photo while we were visiting the Grand Teton National Park. The rear cover photo was taken in Roswell, NM. She is responsible for many of the photos throughout this book.

I'd like to thank Airstream Inc. Without Airstream, we wouldn't have all of these wonderful vintage trailers to restore. Over the years, Airstream has been very gracious toward the Vintage Airstream Podcast. They've even granted interviews, including one with the CEO, Bob Wheeler. They have given permission for us to reprint the Airstream Trailer Weights located in Appendix B. This document lists the weights and lengths for trailers from 1954–2010.

I'd also like to recognize Rob Baker and Colin Hyde. These two gentlemen, who are admittedly infected with aluminitus (an uncontrollable urge to owning vintage Airstreams), share their Airstream knowledge, experience, and insight. Not only have they shared their knowledge on the show, but also in person to anyone who needs their help. They are true Airstreamers in every sense of the word. Without them, the VAP would never have been possible.

I'd like to thank Frank Yensan, who was always willing to step in as a personality on the show. Frank filled in whenever the show needed him. We're grateful. Frank is a listener who restored his own trailer, and whose love of aluminum turned into a restoration business of his own. You can find out more about Frank's business at his website: www.frankstrailerworks.com.

I would like to thank the folks at vintageairstream.com who have allowed us to use information from the site as research for the book. Vintageairstream.com is a great resource for anyone interested in the hobby.

Thanks to Tom Numelin of PerfectPolish.com who provided polishing photos.

A big thanks to Dave McCrostie who heard my subtle cry for help on *Episode 168: The Do Over*, when I asked for someone to help edit my book project. Dave volunteered and treated the project very professionally throughout the process. I know it took a lot of his personal time. It's very much appreciated.

Table of Contents

Introduction

In July of 2001 I purchased my first vintage Airstream, a 1971 Safari. I didn't know it then, but it was a basket case. I knew it needed work, but I didn't know the vintage lingo at the time. The '71 Safari is a 23-foot trailer, and mine was setup with a rear wet-bath, mid twin beds, and living room up front. At the time we had just two kids, and the 23-foot trailer just barely met the needs of our small family.

The Safari was in really bad shape. The early 70's Airstream trailers have what are called 'wing windows' on the front. These windows are curved from the front to the sides of the trailer, and are notorious for shattering while the trailer is being towed. These windows were no different as they were already shattered and missing, with pieces of sheet metal taped to the rather large vacancies that remained. At least I didn't have to mess with the broken glass. It was just *one* little thing I didn't have to deal with. There would be many more challenges ahead.

Excitement about the prospect of owning an Airstream allowed me to overlook the metal patches duct-taped to the front of the trailer and venture inside. There was yellow shag carpeting, faded laminate countertops, plastic bulkheads(walls front and rear), and cabinets in dark walnut. Every appliance was broken, and the plumbing leaked like a sieve. But, for whatever reason, none of this mattered. After all, it was an *Airstream*. Everyone wants an Airstream.

Over the next several months, I set out to fix up this vintage Airstream, so we could get her back on the road. At the time, restoration resources were difficult to find, and like most would-be restorers, I turned to the Internet for help. There were forum sites for trailers and some personal restoration blogs. If you searched you could get help, but it was a lot of work finding anything meaningful. You never really knew if you were getting good advice.

After we'd used the trailer for a few years, I had the idea for the Vintage Airstream Podcast, better known as 'theVAP'. I wanted the theVAP to be a direct line for people who had questions on restoring their Airstream.

Podcasting was fairly new at the time, most people had never heard of it.   Not only would I have to educate Airstreamer's about what a podcast was, I'd have to find two Panel Pros willing to take a chance of being part of one.   I had to find the right people to join me.   As luck would have it, a very enthusiastic Airstreamer, Rob Baker, answered my call.   Rob had just commissioned Colin Hyde, a professional Airstream restorer, to begin a restoration of his 1958 Sovereign of the Road trailer. Both Rob and Colin agreed to be the show's first Panel of Pros.

Colin's industrial and mechanical background, and the fact that he was in the restoration business, made him a perfect Panel Pro.   Rob's infectious love for 'all things aluminum', and fun attitude fit the show perfectly.   The three of us worked great together, answering restoration questions for many years.   We recorded the show over the Internet, and never met in person until years later.   An avid listener, Frank Yensan, joined the ranks and became a Pro as the show progressed through the years.

This book chronicles my life with Airstream trailers, restoring a vintage unit, and how the Vintage Airstream Podcast played an important role in both.   My hope is that reading this book will enlighten you on many aspects of choosing, recovering, restoring, and of course, enjoying your vintage Airstream.

If you're new to trailering, jump ahead to Trailer 101 in Appendix A. That chapter will give you a good understanding of the basics.

As Airstream founder, Wally Byam, might say, "Here's hoping you will be able to use your vintage Airstream to see what's over the hill, and the next one after that."

                              -Tim Shephard
                              The Vintage Airstream Podcast
                              theVAP.com

Chapter One

Falling for Airstream

First Camping Trip

My friend, Ken, purchased a Coleman popup tent trailer and invited us to go camping with him and his family. We'd never camped before, so he kindly loaned us a small dome tent. I'm sure he had good intentions. We packed up our van full of sleeping bags, pillows, a little bit of trepidation, and headed down the road.

After an eight-hour drive to the Northern California redwoods, we arrived at the campground. The drive seemed like it went on forever, and we were happy to finally arrive. Ken picked a campsite far away from any facilities in search of quiet solitude, which is fine if you have your own facilities with you. As we found out in the middle of the night, it's not so good if you're in a tent. I really don't want to go into what happened that night, but you should be able to figure it out.

As it turned out, we learned two lessons that night. The first was that you need a bathroom. The second lesson was about a little thing called condensation. The temperatures dropped into the low forties, and we had water dripping on us in the morning. Definitely not a great start for a family who hadn't camped before. We came to the conclusion that the dome tent was too small for the three of us, and we needed a larger one. The next day, we decided to go to Wal-Mart and buy the biggest tent they had. We found one, and it was huge, it actually had three rooms!

The new tent was an improvement, but when we saw Ken and his family sitting comfortably at the dining table playing cards with overhead lights on in their popup, we realized we were missing out. We were roughing it *too* much. Right then we knew… we were *not* tent campers. After the trip, we promptly returned the tent, and set out to find a popup trailer of our own.

We looked at a few used popups, and soon realized that tent trailers didn't typically have a bathroom. After tent camping, a bathroom was a 'must have', so we expanded our search to travel trailers. I wanted to purchase a used trailer, because I wasn't sure camping was going to be something we really wanted to do. I didn't want to invest too much money in it.

I quickly learned that used travel trailers are usually not in the best of shape. In fact, the ones I saw were rusty, faded, and generally run down. A used trailer was going to need work, and a lot of cash. I had to ask myself, "Was an older trailer worth fixing up, putting lots of labor and money into it?" After more research, I decided it wasn't a worthy investment, as resale values of trailers were very low. There wouldn't be anyway to recover my investment. There had to be a better way...

Going Vintage

I don't remember exactly when I started considering Airstreams. Perhaps it was after I noticed them while going through 'trailer for sale' ads, I really don't remember. Regardless of how I discovered them, they were something I wanted to consider. There were plenty of old Airstreams available too. Although it's funny, when you've found one you're interested in you forget that, and think it's the last one on earth. I didn't recognize them as vintage either. To me they were just old. I did notice that the old Airstreams weren't rusted out like the other brands that I had looked at.

I started researching Airstreams on the Internet, and I found out that people restored them all the time. Not only that, but restoring them *increased* their value. If I invested in fixing up a vintage Airstream (notice it's vintage now that I'm interested), and we decided that we didn't want to continue camping, I could sell the trailer and recover my costs. Perfect!

The first Airstream that we saw was a 20-foot 1968 Globetrotter. The layout contained a couch/bed, which I later learned is called a gaucho. There was a second gaucho next to it forming an L shape. The setup was supposed to sleep four, but it seemed to my wife, Debra, and I that sleeping four would be pretty cramped. At the time there were three of us, with one more on the way. Even so, I thought it could work.

The back of the trailer had a dent the size of a basketball on the outside rear endcap. Somehow, the dent simply didn't matter. I was smitten by the aluminum, and I wanted it right away. I thought, "Who knows when we'll find another one, and the guy said it doesn't leak!" A mantra I would hear over and over about Airstreams. Of course my wife, the voice of reason, suggested that we think about it, and we left without the trailer that day. I let it be known how disappointed I was. Yes, I was whining.

Navigating my way through careful marital negotiations, I successfully talked my wife into buying the Globetrotter that night. I called the seller the next day, but the trailer was gone. They had sold it right after we left. I was not happy, but in the end Debra was right. The layout of the trailer was too small, and the large dent was something I'd never be able to repair. It would have always bothered me.

A short time later, I found a 23-foot 1971 Safari on Craigslist that was only an hour and a half away from our house. I called up the seller, Rick, and made an appointment to see it right away. I mean immediately… I left work to do it. I wasn't about to lose another one!

Rick had purchased the Safari in New Mexico, and towed it up to Northern California to store it inside his airplane hangar. He had hopes of restoring the trailer himself, but he never followed through. During his tow north, the front wing windows shattered. Rick duct-taped large pieces of metal over both of the openings left by the missing windows, which was the first thing I saw when we walked into the hangar. Talk about bad first impressions! When I saw the giant metal 'eye patches' on the trailer, I thought, "Deb isn't going to like this one." We looked inside, and found that everything was there, including a front gaucho, a kitchen area, and mid twin beds. It also had a rear wet-bath. It was *very* 70's with its yellow laminate countertops and lovely yellow shag carpeting! Uh… yeah… lovely.

Debra understandably had concerns, and gently expressed them. After my last disappointment, she knew I would not be leaving without this trailer. It must have been that women's intuition thing we keep hearing about. Not only did I buy the trailer, but I was able to persuade Rick to sell me his hitch too, and he was nice enough to show me how to use it. We took that Safari home with us that very day. This was the first time I had ever towed anything!

I brought home my vintage Airstream. I was now an *Airstreamer*.

My Own Vintage Airstream

1971 Safari with "Eye patches"

The next day after the dust settled, I set out to see what I had parked next to my house. At that moment reality struck. What had I actually brought home, and what would I do with it?

A quick look around revealed what I had gotten myself into, a very old hunk of junk, with tons of potential. What comes next in a few short paragraphs describes some of the work that was done. The work took several months and several do-overs.

It's funny how we always go after the superficial repairs first, and I was no different. Later I learned that taking care of important items like frame repairs, running gear, and brakes, should take precedence. Instead, I took care of some miscellaneous items, like removing the original orange gaucho padding and having them reupholstered by a local shop.   They also made matching curtains for us, after the cheap horizontal blinds I installed turned yellow and fell apart.

I ripped out the yellow shag carpeting, keeping only a small piece in a closet for nostalgia.   I installed 12x12 self-adhesive tiles, which initially worked, but over time they worked loose, and developed gaps that held dirt.   We eventually upgraded to click-together wood flooring that was much nicer.   I recommend hard flooring that can be swept out easily, because a lot of dirt gets tracked inside while camping.   I have seen mobile carpet cleaning vans at campgrounds before, no joke!

The plumbing system had a couple of leaks where a previous owner repaired burst copper pipes with rubber hoses and clamps. I replaced his hoses with my hoses, and they worked for a little while. Again, I should have done it right the first time. In the end I replaced all the plumbing with CPVC. CPVC is chlorinated polyvinyl chloride, basically a type of PVC piping system made for hot and cold potable (drinkable) water use. These days, most people would use PEX tubing for a restoration.

You might have noticed that I had several 'do-overs'.   I installed cheap blinds that faded and fell apart, put in an easy flooring system with cheap tiles that came loose, and added more patch repairs of the plumbing instead of doing a proper repair. Take my advice and spend a little more money *and* time to do it right the first time, or you *will* end up doing it again.

I ventured outside the Safari and found that the top of the roof had the oddest air conditioner I'd ever seen. It was a large steel box with no vent holes of any kind, obviously it was a custom made cover. The cover was secured with about 100 rivets, or so it seemed as I was removing them. It's a good thing I went through all the work to take the cover off, because what I found underneath was the mere *remnants* of an air conditioner.   There were bent pieces of metal, motors, and wiring everywhere! A previous owner must have run into a low hanging branch, because they sure did a number on the poor air conditioner. I'm glad that I checked it before trying to turn it on, who knows what would have happened! I eventually installed a new one, complete with a drain pan and drain tube. Drain pans are important for Airstreams, because they keep the condensation from the air conditioner from randomly dripping down the side of the trailer leaving streaks. Regardless of whether you plan to install an air conditioner, prepare for it by installing a drain tube and a 20-amp circuit for one. You may change your mind on a 100-degree day.

The refrigerator was shot like everything else, so I had to replace it. Refrigerator dimensions changed over the years, so a new one would not fit in the same space as the original. To make a new refrigerator fit and look right, I had to modify the cabinetry and build a new countertop. Changing one countertop in the kitchen, led to having to do the bathroom vanity so they would match. Renovating a vintage trailer is a lot like peeling back an onion, it has many layers, and it will make you cry!

I could go on and on but in short it needed a new battery, charging system, tires, and a water pump. Finally, we were ready to go on our maiden voyage.

Safari's Maiden Voyage

One year after bringing home the 'basket case', the Safari was ready to roll! As the newest Airstreamers of Northern California, we were ready to hit the road. We decided to go to a full-hookup campground, so that we could test out all the trailer's features. A campground in Truckee, CA had our name on it. I never really backed a trailer up before except at the house once, so I was worried about having to do it at the campground. I even feared having to buy gas with the trailer hooked up to the truck. For years after our first trip, we only camped within the radius of a full tank of gas from the house, so I wouldn't have to negotiate the trailer around any gas pumps. My cross-country 'Recovery Mission' cured me of that! I still don't like to back into a space though.

Luck was on my side when we arrived at the campground in Truckee, I got a pull-through site. No backing up required, but the sites were terrible. They were so close together that the slide-out from the camper next door to us was only a foot or two away from our trailer. But hey, we had full hookups!

The campground had problems with their bathroom facilities. It looked like it was time to test out our wet-bath, so I headed out to light the water heater. I had a little trouble getting it to light even though I had tested it at home before we left. After a few tries I finally got it to light. The water heater was the original 31-year-old Bowen that came with the trailer from the factory, which worked for a few showers, but ended up going out on us. I remember writing in my camping journal that we had to microwave bath water for our five-month old daughter.

By the way, I recommend keeping a camping journal of your trips. It's nice to sit down and read and reminisce about what happened on your journeys. Here is the entry from our first camping trip in our Airstream:

Location: Coachland RV Park, Truckee, CA
Date: 7-23-2002
Nights Stay: 2
Price: $34 a night with AAA
Son: 12 yr.

Daughter: 5 mo.

First time we used the trailer. We had full hookups. It's a good thing we did because the campground only had one bathroom, which was broken. So we had to shower in the trailer.

The campground was home to many regulars who lived there year round.

We used it as a starting point to go to North Lake Tahoe and the Ponderosa.

Had a problem with the water heater and had to microwave the bath water for the baby.

We enjoyed the two nights of trailer camping, in spite of the water heater problems. In fact, we enjoyed them so much we wanted to add a third night, but the campground didn't have anything available. So we ventured down to South Lake Tahoe. It was a nice scenic drive along the West Lake Tahoe shore. We drove through Kings Beach and past Emerald Bay. There were a few hairpin turns, but it wasn't too bad of a drive. We found a campground in South Lake Tahoe for a third night, but I was not so lucky there, because I had to back the trailer into the spot! Lets see, I put my hand on the bottom of the wheel. To make the back of the trailer go left, turn the wheel left... I got this! After several minutes we were in our spot. My antics backing up were only mildly entertaining for onlookers. I noticed after parking the trailer, there was only about eight inches of clearance to a pine tree. Oddly enough it wasn't a problem, I didn't have a working awning anyway.

My first time backing into a campsite. Mighty close to that tree!

One interesting event happened while in South Lake Tahoe. We smelled what we thought was a propane gas leak. I checked all of my equipment and everything looked good, so I called the office and told them we smelled propane. They drove up in an *electric* golf cart to look for a propane leak, wow genius. I guess they've never thought of electric sparks igniting propane fumes. They first suspected my 31-year-old very oxidized-clear-coat-peeling trailer. After they cleared me, we noticed just a few sites over there was a motorhome with the hood up, and about three guys looking inside the engine compartment. That's always a good sign (smirk)! When I walked over there I saw that the battery was clearly overheating. It was hot, bulging, and spewing its gaseous smell. I strongly suggested they unplug the camper until they could get this figured out.

I found it interesting that they immediately suspected my Airstream! Hey, looks *can* be deceiving. Honestly, the way it looked, I would have suspected it too!

Outgrowing the Safari

Over the next few months I worked on the Safari. I replaced the bad Bowen water heater with a new Atwood model.   I even replaced the front gaucho with a custom built dining table that converted into a double bed, and I spent over 150 hours polishing the trailer to a mirror finish. With my trailers beautiful shine, no one would rush to check my trailer for a gas leak again!

We were able to get many years of use out of our vintage Airstream. We visited many areas around California including Yosemite, Gilroy, Columbia, Fort Bragg, Duncan Mills, Santa Cruz, and more of Lake Tahoe.   The camping experience is much more than the places we visited, it's the things we experienced and memories we made. We got to pan for gold, visit waterfalls, walk through botanical gardens, and even climb aboard Howard Hugh's Spruce Goose. The trips may have lasted only a few days, but the memories are for a lifetime.

Last trip in the Safari.

Over the years, we outgrew our lovely 23-foot home. We had a third child on the way, and desired a larger trailer. Yes, by this time we were not only full-fledged "*trailerites*"… We were indeed, Airstreamers.

We needed to sell our Safari, and buy a larger Airstream. Now it was time to see if the great experiment worked. If you remember at the beginning of our story, we invested in a vintage Airstream hoping we'd be able to recoup our investment in case we wanted to sell it. We hoped that we could get most of our money back if camping wasn't our thing. In the end, it not only worked out, but we found that we love trailering! I had never considered the need to sell just to buy again. It's funny how things turn out.

We'd invested about $9,000 into our '71 Safari, including the purchase price and the repairs and upgrades that I did over the years. I decided to put the trailer up on eBay to see if we could get our investment back. After our 10-day auction we were happy to see the trailer sell for $12,500. Our experiment had worked out for us in more ways than one. Now we had a down payment for our new trailer.

The day the new owner came to pick up the Safari was a busy one, and came with mixed feelings. The trailer had been a part of our lives for four years, and it took us on many adventures. Selling the trailer was hardest on my daughter. She was four years old at the time, and she had been camping in it since she was five months old. I still have a vivid memory of my baby girl crying as the trailer was towed away for the last time.

Chapter Two

Time for a New Old Trailer

Birth of the VAP

In 2005 I started hearing about a new kind of media on the Internet called a podcast. A podcast is an Internet based radio program where listeners can subscribe to the show using an application like Apple's iTunes. When new episodes are available they are downloaded automatically, so they can listen to the show on their computer or a portable player.

In the beginning, podcasts were mostly technical orientated for computer geeks and hobbyists. Since I'm an Airstream geek, *and* a computer geek, I thought it would be a great idea to combine the two interests. I had restored the '71 Safari myself with some research on the Internet using Airstream related forums and other websites. I thought, "Wouldn't it be great if there was a show where people could call in to ask their questions, and get help with their restoration?" I wish there was something like that around when I was restoring my trailer.

There wasn't an Airstream related podcast at the time, so I thought there was a good chance it would be received well. I had some concerns about using the Airstream name in a website, in case there would be problems with licensing or other legal issues. As it turned out, Airstream Inc. has always been very gracious regarding the show. I knew the program was going to be geared toward restorations, and I liked 'The Vintage Airstream Podcast' as a name, but it was too long for a website plus it had Airstream in it. This led me to 'the VAP'. Since you can't have a space in a website name, it became 'theVAP'. It was a perfect name because theVAP is easy to remember, and enter in a web browser. I registered theVAP.com in August 2005.

Now that I had the name for the show, I needed a format. I always thought of it as a 'car talk' kind of show. I wanted listeners to call or email their questions in, and we'd answer it on the program. I came up with the idea of having a Panel of Professionals, who would be Airstreamers that were proficient in restoration. The idea was simple enough. The Pros would be on the show with me to answer questions from our listeners. In addition to Panel Pros, I originally wanted to have Field Agents who'd be listeners with specific Airstream experiences. I would call upon them to answer questions that I would receive from listeners via email or voicemail. The Field Agents would record their answer, so that I could play it back on the show during final editing. It was essential to have audio for playback since the VAP is a radio program. The Field Agents idea never materialized, but the Panel Pros idea stuck from the beginning of the show to this very day.

In order to find some Panel Pros I sent a request on an Airstream email list. The only response I received was from an eager Rob Baker. Rob is the kind of guy you would want for a show like this, because he's personable, funny, and enthusiastic about Airstreams. Rob explained that he had recently purchased a 1958 Airstream, and was going to have Colin Hyde restore it. Rob thought that Colin might be interested in doing the show, as he was just starting a restoration business, and it would be good publicity.

Colin was a little cautious about the idea, because he didn't fully understand what a podcast was, and wasn't very computer literate. He's strictly a hardware guy, as in steel and aluminum not computers. Colin has a great mechanical background and wonderful communications skills. He can explain complex concepts and make them understandable. He is also brutally honest about restoration work, even if it's something you may not want to hear.

Rob and Colin live on the East coast, and I'm on the West coast, which means all of our communication was done over the Internet via email and online chats. In the beginning, I would send an outline of the show, complete with questions and topics so they could prepare for the show. After we had a few years under our belts, I stopped sending outlines because they just weren't needed anymore.

We recorded the episodes every other Thursday night. After the recording I'd edit the show, adding in the opening theme song, and removing any dead air. Then I'd upload the show to the website, and make it available to the listeners.

We tackled many topics that first year including; Airstream construction, trailer recovery missions, restoration vs. refurbishment, and more. It's amazing that after seven years there are still topics to discuss.

We do hear similar questions now and again, but we keep in mind that there are always new folks listening to us.

Since our show is Internet based, anyone in the world can download it. I was surprised to learn that we are heard in over 22 countries worldwide. Of course, I'll admit, some countries may only have one listener. Still amazing to us.

Frank Yensan was an avid listener of the show and an Airstream owner. Frank would be one of the first ones downloading each new show. He'd call in his questions to keep us fed with topics, and encourage others to do the same. After about five years Rob needed a break, so Frank filled his shoes as a Panel Pro. He was always available and eager to help when we needed him.

As time went on, both Rob and Frank left the show for various reasons. Their contributions to the program are some of the best the Internet has to offer. The advantage that a podcast has over a radio show is that the episodes live on forever in our archives as will Rob and Frank's voices on the VAP.

As of this writing we are coming upon our eighth year of broadcasting. That's quite a feat for a podcast or any radio program for that matter. I believe that my original goal has been achieved successfully. We receive a lot of feedback from our listeners who talk about how the show has helped them with their vintage projects.

Way back in May of 2006, we recorded *Episode 19: The Polishing Show*. That show has a very specific memory for me, as it's the episode I mentioned that I was selling my '71 Safari. I was the host of a vintage Airstream program, but I wanted a larger and *newer* trailer. After recording the VAP for nine months, I was not going to own a vintage Airstream anymore. During that show Colin said, "There is a dissenter in our midst", and he was right…

A Dissenter In Our Midst

Debra and I loved our vintage Airstream, but we needed to upgrade to a larger trailer. We needed it to sleep five and Airstream had some nice late model 1990's and early 2000's models that fit the bill. I knew that buying another vintage trailer would be a lot of work, and a considerable amount down time. I reasoned that buying a late model Airstream would allow us to keep camping. It made sense to me, but not to Colin and Rob after they found out about my plans during the show.

Most of the time before we record a show we chat a bit, and the same held true for *Episode 19: The Polishing Show*. I mentioned to Colin and Rob that I had my '71 Safari currently listed on eBay for sale, and that I wanted to buy a newer model. The guys *really* gave me a hard time for my decision. After all, they were Panel Pros on the *Vintage* Airstream Podcast, it's their job to be vintage snobs.

We started recording the program like we always did, and I had no intention of telling the audience what I was doing. It wasn't exactly a secret, but it wasn't something I was ready to discuss. Colin and Rob had other ideas. This show was supposed to be about how to polish your trailer, but Colin and Rob kept making not-so-subtle jokes at my expense during the recording. Rob would say something about one of his trailers like, "It's a 1960 Tim, one of the *good* years…" Colin would add, "…and you can polish it to a mirror shine, unlike the newer trailers." I knew they both had smirks on their faces by the tone in their voices. I realized the listener's would have no idea of what we were talking about, so during the show I let the cat out of the bag, and went public about selling my vintage Airstream. I explained why I wanted a newer, non-vintage unit. I spoke about not wanting to restore another trailer, and that I wanted to be able to keep camping without the interruption a restoration would cause. The guys kept after me, and man, they were relentless! They explained that the newer trailer would be double the weight of a vintage model, and harder to polish. At one point Colin said that there was, "A dissenter in our midst" meaning me, the host! Rob said I was "Going to the dark side!"

During the episode we joked on the air about me doing a restoration of a vintage trailer as part of the show. More ribbing from the guys off the air really got me to thinking, "Maybe they are right. Maybe I should stay vintage. Na, I don't want to have to deal with all the work. A new trailer is for me…"

Then There Were Two

I started looking online at late model Airstreams. I was determined to get a trailer so we could keep camping. Debra and I had the opportunity to look at an early '90's Airstream, and it was only an hour drive from our home. Deb liked the trailer, but she was her usual cautious self about it. I wasn't nearly as eager to buy it as I was when we bought the Safari.

There was just something about this Airstream that didn't seem right. It *felt* heavy. I don't mean kinda heavy. I mean *really* heavy. As I looked around the inside, I noticed the solid-surface countertops, thick oak cabinets, and the heavy carpeting on the walls. I couldn't help but think about how hard this would be to tow. This *wide body* Airstream would cause my truck to guzzle the gas!

As I continued my inspection outside, everything on this trailer seemed to be a mystery. I realized that I had no idea how they ran the sewer pipes or the electrical services. How would I be able to repair it? I remember after restoring my '71 Safari that I could repair anything on it.

The final issue was the price. They were asking $23,000. I'm sure it was a fair price, but our hearts just weren't into it, so we left without regrets.

A short time later a second trailer became available, a 1994 Airstream Excella that I found online. I remember it had a too-good-to-be-true price tag. It was a 30-foot model with the layout we wanted, and a dealer was selling it for $14,000. There were only two problems with it. The first problem is that the trailer was located in El Paso, TX, which is about 1,200 miles away. The second problem was that it was supposedly sold. The dealer told me that there was a couple coming to pick it up. I offered him my number in case things didn't work out, but I knew it wasn't very likely at that price.

A few days later the dealer called me back and said, "The wife didn't like it because the closet space was too small." He went on to tell me that the trailer was still available if I wanted it. Of course I did! I asked him to hold it until I got there, because I was coming from California. He agreed. I discussed it with Debra and we thought with the kids in school, it would best that I ask my dad to go with me instead of making it a family trip.

My dad and I headed out the next morning. I think we pulled into El Paso on the third day. At first sight of the dealership I thought, "Uh oh, we're in trouble". It was a small rinky-dink place, and the Airstream that I was interested in was the *only* Airstream in the lot. I immediately got out and started walking around the trailer examining it from every angle. I noticed several things right away. A couple of windows were poorly replaced, and had silicone all over them. I also found body damage, which was poorly repaired by placing a sheet of aluminum over top of the dented panel. Right about this time I knew, I wasn't going to buy this trailer. Not enough closet space? Yeah right…

As the salesman walked out to greet us, he had sort of a gleam in his eye that seemed to say, "I'm going to sell you this trailer!" I was thinking, "Not a chance buddy!" Even so we'd driven all this way, I decided we might as well see the inside. What I saw when we went inside was nearly as bad as the outside. The interior didn't seem very solid, and the dealer didn't have the history of the trailer. On further examination, I saw loose fitting cabinets, loose hull liner (the fabric that's glued to the walls), and general filth. The biggest problem was that the bulkhead walls on the street side were no longer connected to the roof, and the interior sliding doors were crooked. Then it dawned on me, this trailer had been in some kind of accident. That's why the last couple didn't buy it. That's why it's selling for half of the going rate. That's why it *kept becoming* available.

I told the dealer, thanks, but no thanks. Yes, I had driven 1,200 miles to look at a trailer for ten minutes and leave. I couldn't believe it either, but it was the right decision.

Maybe Colin and Rob were right, these newer trailers just weren't cutting it. Maybe I should go back to vintage.

Vintage vs. New

Why would anyone one want an old trailer anyway? I originally chose to 'go vintage' because I wanted to get into trailering inexpensively. Where there better reasons that that? I wanted to understand why some people would *choose* to have an older trailer over a new one.

Why would someone buy a 100-year-old home, or a car from the 1950's? Things that are older have a certain character or charm about them. They were made in a simpler time with simpler technology. A lot of the components were hand-crafted. This in itself doesn't make them better than new, but for a certain type of individual it does. They can look beyond the dilapidation and see the potential.

Think of a vintage Airstream as a blank canvas. One that you can paint your own picture on, and create whatever vision you personally have. You can restore a vintage trailer to showroom condition of yesteryear, or you can update it to something new that suits you. The problem you have when looking at a new trailer is that you're saddled with someone else's idea of what you might like. You have to compromise from the start.

When you choose to restore a vintage Airstream, you're essentially restoring history. By restoring a trailer you're not adding to a landfill, but saving something from it. As I mentioned earlier, it does require a certain type of individual. Someone interested in restoring an Airstream needs to look past the issues of an 'As-Found' trailer and see its potential. Patience and perseverance are words that come to mind when you choose to 'go vintage'. Once you commit to restoring a vintage Airstream, you have an open canvas. There will be hurdles to overcome, guaranteed, it's all part of the journey. You'll also have great satisfaction when you're camping in a trailer that you restored. Often times when camping in our restored trailer, I look around and think about all the work I put into the restoration. It gives me a great sense of accomplishment knowing that we are enjoying the product of my labor.

There are many advantages to 'going vintage'. One advantage is that you can select the type and quality of the appliances, furnishings, and layout that you like. Almost anything that you can imagine can be on the table.   Another advantage is that many of the older Airstreams used a higher quality of aluminum that has an alclad coating, which is stronger and more resilient than modern Airstreams. Vintage Airstreams are lighter and often have better layouts than newer models that allow you to see all the way through the trailer, from the front window to the rear window while towing.   There is a lower entry price when buying vintage, which you can add to as funds become available.   Don't forget that vintage Airstreams can be polished to a mirror shine. Folks, let's face it, vintage Airstreams are cool!

Ok, I got it, going vintage is the way the go. The next step is to find the right vintage canvas.

Chapter Three

Choosing Vintage

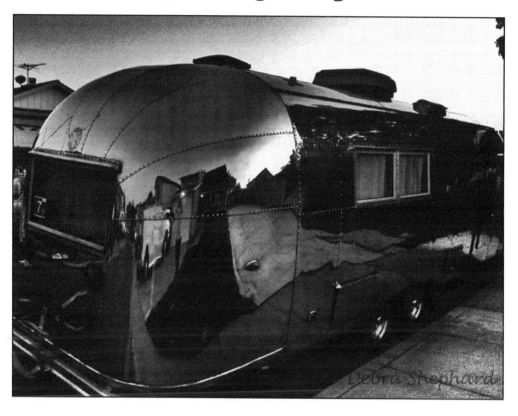

Choosing My Vintage

After receiving my reprimand from Colin and Rob, I decided to stay vintage. Deep down I knew they were right. 'Going vintage' means different things to different people. To me it meant that after I restored it, I could repair and service it. It also meant that I could recover my investment if I decided to sell it. I had first hand experience in doing that from selling my Safari, which was going to fund the new trailer. Now that I knew I was going to stay vintage, the next step was to figure out what *style of vintage*.

Choosing the right trailer for my current and future needs was very important to me. After all, this was a major project I was about to embark on, and I only wanted to do it once. Well, in my case, twice. There are a lot of things to consider that I'll cover in this chapter. I was lucky to have four years of experience owning a vintage trailer, and almost a year of show experience to aid in my decisions. Both of these were very helpful.

It was time to start thinking about what we wanted in a new trailer. Since our family had grown, we need it to have sleeping for at least five people. One thing came up regularly when we used the Safari is that we didn't like the wet-bath. A wet-bath is a bathroom where the whole room becomes a shower; there's no bathtub. A big downside to a wet-bath is that the entire room gets wet when you shower, and if you don't dry the floor completely after each use it gets dirty fast. If you have some dirt or sand on your shoes and step on the wet floor of the bathroom, you get instant mud. I understand the purpose of having a wet-bath, because it makes good use of space in a small trailer. Now I get to *choose* not to have one, and that's exactly what I was going to do.

The Safari has some custom parts that were designed just for the trailer and were difficult to repair. I already mentioned the front curved glass on the wing windows. I had to make replacements from polycarbonate, which worked, but it wasn't ideal. The bathroom vanity was custom molded plastic that turned to a dull yellow color and somewhat faded. There are ways to restore them, but it's a custom item that needed to be cared for. The Safari has tambour cabinet doors, which are similar to what's used on a roll-top desk. These doors always jammed and were extremely difficult to repair. I wanted to concentrate on trailers that didn't have as many custom parts. This requirement alone led me to the '50's and early '60s trailers.

I really wanted real wood in the new trailer. The Safari had laminated plastic cabinets and bulkheads in a very dark walnut color. The cabinets were durable, but they didn't do much in the esthetics department. I never cared for the dark walnut in such a small area like the inside of a trailer, and I thought that lighter colors would open it up more. In the end, I didn't get the color I wanted, but I did get real wood.

Now we had our requirements. The trailer should be longer than 23-feet, with enough room to sleep five people. It should have real wood, the least amount of custom parts as possible, and a large bathroom including a separate shower or tub.

I wasn't too concerned about the condition of the trailer, since I knew that I was going to be replacing everything in it anyway. As I look back at it today, I'm not sure why I was so confident. I think Colin and Rob created some kind of reality distortion field around me! Speaking of replacing everything, there are a lot of people who prefer to have original appliances. I'm *not* one of them. I prefer modern technology and comfort. If you want to keep that 50-year-old refrigerator going and fiddle with getting it to light every season, go ahead. I'll give you the bragging rights for sure. As for me, I'm going to push a button. I fully intended to modernize the trailer as much as possible during the restoration. I wanted to have a vintage trailer that rolled of the 2009 assembly line.

I also needed to remember that I didn't have to buy the first trailer I looked at. It was hard for me though. This is actually a personality trait I have. Some may even call it a flaw. I can get *very* focused on something and it becomes the center of my universe until I acquire it. The search for a vintage Airstream was like that. Every trailer I looked at seemed like it was going to be the last one I'd ever find. There was one trailer that I wanted to stay away from. One trailer that we hear about on theVAP *over* and *over* again. One trailer that frightens even the most experienced Airstreamer, the *dreaded* 'Polished Turd'.

The Polished Turd

There is one kind of trailer anyone looking for a used Airstream needs to know about. Regular listeners of the VAP have no doubt heard the term, Polished Turd. This type of trailer not only exists, but it's something you should be very careful to avoid.

A Polished Turd is a vintage Airstream that the seller has polished the outside, while the inside has *not* been restored. It's human nature to see the beautiful exterior and assume the interior is just as nice. That's not always the case. In fact, many times it's not.

Someone new to vintage Airstreams might see a nicely polished trailer and assume that the entire trailer has been properly restored. Why wouldn't they? If you build a house, you start with the foundation, not the paint. These vintage newbies may end up paying top dollar thinking they are getting a restored trailer. They don't realize there is a problem until *after* they buy it at the inflated price, and things start to fall apart on them. The allure of a nicely polished Airstream is huge, but you need to dig deeper and see what you are really getting for your money. Sites like eBay and Craigslist are notorious for having Polished Turd trailers. The sellers may not even know what they are selling. As with all things in life, buyers beware.

In reality, a properly restored trailer will cost many tens of thousands of dollars. As a new vintage wannabe, you don't know this yet. You may decide to pay $10,000 for a Polished Turd that's only worth $3,000. You'll think you got a deal because you didn't pay $70,000 for the *other* shiny-restored trailer that was for sale. The difference is that *you* just bought a Polished Turd.

Polished Turds can hold many secrets. Often times they will have rotted subfloors. Sometimes the seller will lay a new floor *over* the bad one, and they will point out because they don't fall through the floor, it's structurally sound. A solid floor is a vital component of an Airstream.

Rotted and rusted out frames go hand in hand with bad subfloors. Years of wet insulation pressed up against the steel frame takes its toll. Airstream's enclosed underbelly hides much of this problem and makes it hard to inspect. This is where documentation becomes important. A properly restored trailer will have photos of the frame and belly work that was done.

Appliances often get overlooked. Ovens and furnaces may look pristine because they are not used very often, yet they still can go bad over forty or fifty years. You may find that other appliances may or may not work, or the owner might say, "It worked the last time we tried it", which could have been ten years ago! A failed refrigerator can be an expensive lesson.

Hosting the VAP taught me how to avoid the Polished Turd. How can *you* avoid the Polished Turd trailer? You need to educate yourself on how to inspect a vintage trailer. Believe me, I know you want to buy the first trailer you see, I understand, I was the same way. You *must* resist buying the first one, even though it may seem like it's the only one on Earth. I'm here to tell you that there are many vintage Airstreams available.

When you get the opportunity to look at one, try and take a more experienced friend with you to help you understand what you're looking at. If you find an Airstream that you are really interested in, arrange to have it inspected by a vintage restoration professional.

It's extremely rare to find a restored trailer for sale with the restoration fully documented with photos and receipts. In over ten years of Airstreaming I have not seen one, and the reason is simple. Restoring a trailer is a huge commitment that takes a great deal of time, energy, and money. The process of a restoration is, by nature, a personal experience, because you build the trailer to what *you* desire. If you do it right, it will be the last trailer you'll ever need.

The point of this chapter is to make you think. Don't get caught up in a buying frenzy, and be careful not to pay for more than you're getting. It can be a very expensive lesson that will leave a bad taste in your mouth, not a great way to start this journey.

Search by Era

Now that you know to avoid the Polished Turd, it's time to start thinking about what you want in a vintage Airstream. Airstream has been in production since 1931. There was a little break during the war, but for the most part they have been in business for over eighty years. That's a *lot* of trailers to choose from.

Back in *Episode 1,* we talked about narrowing your selection by era or decade. Searching by decade makes good sense, I really like this idea. Each decade has its advantages and disadvantages; they are pretty distinct. Limiting my search based on the era of the trailer helped me to pinpoint the right one for my family. I wanted a longer trailer with a real wood interior. These two items alone helped narrowed it down quite a bit.

Each decade has differences that may interest you. As you read over the following descriptions of the decades, I want you to keep something in mind. Any trailer that you pick is going to need the *same* basic set of repairs. Of course I'm speaking in general here, but every trailer will need: new subfloors, frame repairs, axles, appliances, tanks, and much more. It's important to start with the trailer that you really want. You may think that you are saving money by buying a *newer* vintage trailer, but these trailers are still twenty, thirty, and even forty years old. They will all have similar issues that will need to be addressed. Take your time learning about the different models. Don't settle here, it's critical.

The 1930's: The pre-World War II trailers, including those from 1936 to 1938, are very rare. There are some that still exist and have been restored. These very early trailers are not much more than an aluminum tent. They don't have much in the way of today's amenities that most people would expect a trailer to have. Finding a restoration candidate of this era would be difficult.

The 1940's: Airstream produced five models in the 1940's. They include the 16-foot Wee Wind, 19-foot Trailwind, 22-foot Liner, 24-foot Limited, and the 28-foot Whirlwind. The 40's era trailers had pipe frames, so most of the trailers in this vintage will require new frames to be built. On the show, we always recommend upgrading to new frames at the time of the restoration. The rarity of these trailers will make it difficult to find replacement parts. The front curved window is one example of a rare part. We discussed the '30's and '40's on *Episode 30: The 30's and 40's*.

The 1950's: The '50's starts the first full decade of models built after the war. There are many lengths from the 15-foot Cruisette to the 32-foot Liner. We start to see a more complete range of amenities including water heaters, full baths, and kitchens. This era, like the '60's, used real wood for the cabinetry. Weight mattered back then, so everything was built as light as possible. For example, a mid '50's trailer that's 26-foot long has a dry weight of only 3300 lb. A similar model from early 2000 that's 25-foot has a dry weight of *over* 6000 lb. That's almost double the weight for a shorter trailer! Be sure to catch *Episode 37: The 50's*, when we discuss this decade of trailer with Airstream historian, Fred Coldwell.

The 1960's: The '60's era is widely considered to be the last decade that offered a true 'Byam trailer'. Wally Byam, the founder of Airstream, passed away in 1962. Although the designs of the '60's certainly had the same influences from the founder as the earlier models, many vintage Airstreamer's take a certain pride in owning a pre-1962 trailer. This was the last decade to use real wood for the cabinetry. In the early '60's, much like the '50's, most of the hardware and fixtures are still commonly found in hardware stores. Window glass, for example, is easy to find and replace. Much of the mechanical hardware or at least reproductions are readily available. As the decade continued, more custom parts were created to speed construction and lower costs. These items include custom molded bathroom vanities and sinks that will have to be restored. The '60s was also the last decade of the door-within-a-door, which is a characteristic that is unique to vintage Airstreams, and is a nice engineering feat not attempted today. 1960 was the last year of the leaf-spring axles, which was replaced by the Dura-Torque axle the following year. We talked about the '60's in *Episode 58: The 60's*.

Coveted door-within-a-door.

The 1970's: Beginning in '71, Airstream started using laminate cabinets and bulkheads.   Gone were the days of real wood veneer cabinets.   Curved front windows started to appear along with custom made interior parts like molded sinks, vanities, and endcaps. This decade does retain the alclad aluminum of the earlier models.   Alclad is a coating that is manufactured on the aluminum panels that adds a great deal of strength.   Airstream produced a promotional video that shows a sheet of alclad coated-aluminum supporting a trailer's tongue. When the same feat was performed on an untreated sheet, the aluminum tore in half!

This is the decade that grey tanks were introduced to Airstreams. Some '73 models have grey tanks, but generally they were available in '74. Prior to '74, any grey water, the byproduct of sinks and showers, just ran straight to the dump outlet bypassing the black tank valve.   An unsuspecting trailer owner could find himself with a tub full of... well... let's just say an unwelcome surprise if the sewer drain ever backed up!

In 1967 Airstream approved a merger with Beatrice Foods. Beatrice brought some capitol that the company needed that allowed for modern manufacturing processes and other technologies that would end up in the '70's trailers. Many '70's trailers suffer from 'tail droop or sag' and some people blame Beatrice for these issues.   Others feel that it was the addition of the grey tanks without properly engineered frame upgrades. Colin, Rob, and I believe that when you throw worn axles and rotted sub-floors into the mix you're asking for trouble. Despite these issues, the '70's trailers benefitted from many upgrades relative to earlier designs. They can be polished to a mirror shine, and are probably the most economical way to 'go vintage'.

Visit Rallies

It always helps to see trailers in person. There's just something about walking through a vintage trailer that makes a difference than just looking at photos. I attended a couple of rallies in Northern California with my Safari, and visited some just as a day trip. It was very enlightening seeing how people setup and used their Airstream.

The great thing about vintage Airstreams is that they are often gathered together all around the country at rallies. There are a few clubs out there that hold regular rallies throughout the year, and all over the country. It shouldn't be too hard to find one close enough to visit.

The first club that comes to mind is the Wally Byam Caravan Club International. In 1955 followers of the founder, Wally Byam, created the Wally Byam Caravan Club, now called the WBCCI. The Wally Byam Caravan Club International offers fun, fellowship, and adventure for owners of the world's finest RV, the Airstream. Founded in 1955, the WBCCI has touched the lives of Airstream owners for nearly sixty years and continues in the spirit of Wally Byam, inventor of the Airstream, who introduced glamour to trailer touring. Dedicated to fostering friendships and a passion for travel through a common interest in the Airstream lifestyle, the WBCCI offers caravans, rallies and activities through more than 122 local Units throughout the United States and Canada. Learn more at www.wbcci.org.

Another club that comes to mind is the Tin Can Tourists. The Tin Can Tourists is a club of vintage trailer owners that has been around since 1919. Between the mid '80's through mid '90's, the club faded away and was no longer practicing. In the late '90's the club was renewed and still exists today. The Tin Can Tourists club is different from the WBCCI in that they allow *any* make of vintage trailer in their club, not just Airstreams. However, Airstreams are a big part of their membership simply because Airstreams are one of the most widely available vintage trailers. You can find them on the Internet at www.tincantourists.com.

Once you find a local rally to visit, be sure to attend what is called 'Open House'. Open house usually occurs on a Saturday during the course of the rally, and is the time that owner's open up their trailers and invite anyone interested inside.   Most Airstreamer's are proud of the work they've done restoring their trailer and will freely answer questions about it. This is a great way to see different models of vintage trailers as well as talk with their owners about how they use their trailer and how it works for them. If they allow, it's a good idea to take pictures and note what you are looking at.

Size Matters

The whole journey started for me because I needed a bigger trailer. I had just sold the 23-foot Safari. I was looking to go larger, something like a 26 or 28-foot trailer. That really narrowed my choices for a vintage Airstream. Some people want a short 16-foot Bambi, while others may want the longest 30-foot Sovereign of the Road. That's one of the great things about Airstreams, you have the option to choose either.

One limiting factor on trailer size will certainly be your tow vehicle's capabilities. Never go beyond what the manufacturer of your vehicle states you can tow in weight or trailer length. They build these vehicles, and it's their job to know what it can handle. I will say this, if your vehicle is undersized, and your family really needs a large trailer, get a bigger tow vehicle. I know that this suggestion sounds drastic and it may be. But consider this, you will have your trailer for many years. In fact, you may have it many more years than your current tow vehicle, and you'll likely put more money into the restoration than your tow vehicle is worth. I'm only suggesting that you get the trailer you really need and want now, and possibly rent or borrow a properly sized tow vehicle until its time to purchase a new one. *Never* tow without a properly sized vehicle, but don't let having the wrong tow vehicle keep you from getting the right trailer.

For some reason when people think of Airstream trailers they always picture a short trailer like a 16-foot Bambi or a 17-foot Caravel. These trailers look really great when they're all polished up, and they are very light to tow. The only problem is that they are small, really small. If you are by yourself, it might be the way to go. If however, you are a small family or even just couple, I think you will find it very cramped, very quickly. You need to resist the urge to buy a trailer because it's *cute*. Now is the time to think in terms of function and comfort. Remember, this is a major commitment, one that you will make a long-term investment in. If you think your family will be expanding like mine did, or you might be taking friends with you, consider the size of the trailer now.

In the long run, you will have more room in a longer trailer, even if it's just two of you. Longer trailers are easier to find, and you will probably pay a lower price for one over a shorter trailer. Many of the longer trailers have tandem axles (two axles), which make it a little safer in the event of a tire failure. Another secret to the longer trailers, they are easier to back in. If you're like me you can use all the help you can get!

Just keep these thoughts in mind when searching for a trailer. Most people have never complained about having *too much* room while camping. Trailers are *always* too big to tow while on the road, and too small to camp in once you've arrived at the campground!

Tanks

Back in the early days of trailering there were no tanks or even plumbing for that matter.   The trailers themselves were basically aluminum tents.   Over the years as the technology matured, fresh and black water tanks were introduced.   If you're not familiar with tanks on trailers, refer to the Tanks and Usage in Trailer 101.   You can also listen to *Episode 91: Tank You Very Much*.   In that episode we talk in depth about the different tanks used in vintage Airstreams.

The first fresh water tanks were aluminum cylinders usually located behind the gaucho inside the front of the trailer.   The early tanks were pressurized by a hand pump, and later by an on-board electric air pump. The air pump pressurized the tank, which allowed the water to flow when a faucet was opened.   The nice thing about a pressurized tank system is that whenever you open a faucet you don't have to hear a water pump run like modern trailers.   You also don't always use battery power just to run water.   Often you can re-pressurize the system with a bicycle pump.   Modern trailers use electric water pumps to pump water out of the tank.   These on-demand pumps require a constant source of power when running.   The original aluminum tanks from the 50's and 60's will most likely be corroded and require replacement.   Your options are to have a new metal tank built that can be pressurized, or changing to an on-demand water pump system.   With on-demand water pump systems you can use a plastic fresh water tank, which is more typical these days and is what I did for the Ambassador.

Black tanks in vintage trailers from the '50's and '60's were typically made of fiberglass.   As the years passed, plastic tanks became more common.   Fiberglass tanks are sturdier than plastic tanks and can be repaired more easily.   Original plastic tanks will most likely be cracked and need to be replaced.   It's possible to repair a plastic tank, but it can be a problem in the long run.   Getting the right kind of plastic to weld your repair is difficult and more often than not, if you do manage to repair a crack, another one will surface.   On the show we almost always recommend to have a new tank built to order.

Grey water tanks in vintage Airstreams did not make their way into the trailers until 1974.   Even at that time the tanks were very small, as little as five gallons. In trailers before '74 the grey water was plumbed to the dump connection after the black tank valve. What this means is that grey water ran straight out the drain on the bottom of the trailer. Back in the day, it was permissible to let the grey water run on the ground. These days, letting grey water drain on the ground is frowned upon. You must keep your grey water and dispose of it in the sewer, just like your black water.   External tanks, generally referred to as blue boys, can be connected to the drain connection of a vintage trailer to capture the grey water for dumping later. Blue boys can be purchased in a variety of sizes; smaller is better in this case as they can get extremely heavy when full. Water weights 8.33lbs per gallon, so you can do the math and decide what size tank to purchase. Best practice is to buy one with wheels and a hitch ball attachment so you can actually tow it to a dump. When you rebuild your trailer, you will certainly want to add a grey tank to your plans.

Where to Find it

There are many places to find your vintage trailer. Below are some of the places that I looked before we found our vintage beauty. We ultimately found our 1960 Ambassador on eBay, which I'll talk about in the next chapter.

EBay.com: eBay is an online auction site. When shopping on eBay you have go into it with the right attitude. As long as you know that *everything* on the trailer is going to have to be replaced, you have the right attitude! It's a good thing that I did, because 'looks are deceiving', and they were for me too. The story told on eBay was *far* different from what I saw in person when I picked up my trailer. All too common of an event.

In *Episode 13: eBay Trailering*, we talked about purchasing a trailer on eBay, and what to look out for. One of the things we discussed was to pay particular attention to the photos in the auction. They can be taken in a way that makes things look better than they really are. The seller may only take a photo of the good sections and omit any negatives. Unfortunately, this was true in my case.

Pay close attention to how the seller lists the appliances in the auction. A good indication of trouble is if they mention, "Everything worked the last time we used it." That statement should be a red flag. The listing for our Ambassador is an example of poor information in the auction that stated, "Everything works". One such item was the refrigerator. While the Ambassador had a refrigerator, it was an apartment model that can't be used without an electrical hookup. After I got the trailer home, I found that the refrigerator was broken anyway. You really need to have a RV refrigerator that can operate on propane. A house refrigerator is pretty much useless for a travel trailer, unless you are going to park the trailer and never move it.

Another common description on an eBay auction is, "The floor seems solid". The auction might read, "I'm a 250 lb. guy and it's holding me". Unfortunately, that is no indication of a rot free floor. I'll discuss it more in the Trailer Inspections chapter, but a solid floor, from edge to edge, is very important in an Airstream. Jumping up and down on the middle of the floor means nothing.

Make sure that there are no glaring errors in the listing like the trailer model or year. These indicate that the seller is not very detail orientated in his listing. It maybe a good idea to skip this trailer and keep looking. Also be sure and check the seller's feedback. If there is a lot of negative feedback, move along. If they sell a lot of trailers, they may just be flipping them for a quick buck. Flipping a trailer is when someone buys trailers for next to nothing, just to part them and sell them for profit. Flipping a trailer is not necessarily a bad thing, but more than likely means the seller doesn't know much about it. In addition, they've probably removed a lot of the hard to get parts.

Sellers generally wait for spring to list their trailer on eBay. That's the beginning of camping season, so there will be more trailers to choose from during this time. There will also be more competition during the auction, because more people are looking to buy a trailer.

It's a good idea to keep an eye on the completed listings. In the advance search page on eBay, there is a search box that you can check to show only auctions that have been completed. This will help you find pricing trends, and you can get a feel of the supply and demand for the many different models available. Remember, the smaller trailers usually have a premium price tag because more people are interested in them. For example, you'll have an easier time finding a 24-foot Overlander then a 16-foot Bambi. Luckily for me, I was looking for a longer trailer. Even so, my auction ended up having 32 bids on it.

Keep in mind how far the trailer is from you. If the trailer is too far for you to inspect yourself, try and find someone who can look at the trailer for you and take detailed photos. A long distance 'Recovery Mission' may add considerably to the cost.

Be on your guard when dealing with eBay. It's *your* job to do the homework before you bid. Doing your homework means checking the photos carefully and asking for more photos if you don't have the clarity you desire. Keep your communication through eBay's message system to ask questions. Compare the answers with known information from websites you trust, or what you've heard on the VAP. The seller may not know everything about his trailer, and may honestly think it's in a usable condition. It's your job, as the buyer, to weed out all the missing information. If at all possible, make a trip to inspect the trailer yourself during the auction. If the trailer is too far for you to visit, it maybe worth it to wait for a closer trailer to become available. In most cases you will be paying a premium for a trailer on eBay, because you're bidding against others. The best Airstream find is always next to a barn on the side of the road somewhere when the owner doesn't even know he wants to sell it yet!

EBay is a great place to buy parts, especially hard to find ones. As you go through your restoration you will find that there are some Airstream specific parts you need. You should do daily eBay searches during your restoration to see what items are out there, because the rare parts get snapped up quickly at premium prices. You'll be surprised at how much some parts will go for. An example of this is door handle on my '71 Safari, which can run several hundred dollars. Sometimes eBay is the only place to get a rare part. A good tip is to narrow your search for completed items, just like when searching for trailers. You can find out the history of a specific part, and see what the item sold for in the past, or the last time it was available. Try searching with a misspelling of part you need. I know that sounds like odd advice, but you might get lucky with your search results and lower your competition that way. With patience and persistence, you can find most anything you will need from eBay or other means. It took me three years to find a missing glass cover for my 1960 light fixture. But I have it now, thanks to Rob!

Craigslist.org: Craigslist is like a newspaper's white page listing. There are listings all over the United States, and many sellers put their trailers on craigslist. As with any purchase, you need to be very careful. Unlike eBay's feedback system, you generally do not have anyway to check on the seller to get a feel for their honesty. All Craigslist does is get two individuals together, the buyer and the seller. It's up to you to know what you are buying; you need to keep alert. You're likely to find a trailer locally, or close enough for a nice drive to see the trailer in person for an inspection. Always follow Craigslist's safety warnings when dealing with sellers.

Online Forums: Forum sites online are a good place to buy a trailer. A lot of forums have classified sections just for the purpose of listing trailers and parts for sale. It's good practice to make sure the seller has been a member of the forum for a while, which will help to separate the regular members from the people who join the forum just to unload their problem trailer.

Keep a Lookout: One of the best ways to find a trailer to restore is to just keep an eye out. Look for neglected trailers as you drive by open fields or old barns. Often the owners of these hidden treasures will let them go for a nice price. Since there is no competition, you should be able to get a great deal without too much trouble.

Spread the word to your friends and family that you are looking for a vintage trailer. You may be surprised how many people see them in their daily travels. They might know someone who has a trailer that's been sitting neglected for years, and you might get it for a song.

What Should it Cost?

The street price of vintage Airstreams can very greatly for any number of reasons. The price can be different just because of where the trailer is located in the country, like the East coast vs. the West coast. Other reasons may include the era of the trailer, or a perceived value added by the seller.

If a seller has put some work into the trailer they will want to recover their investment, so it may be better to keep looking for one that has not had any work done to it. This will eliminate any *perceived* added value, and you are in more control of the restoration. I know this sounds backwards, but you don't know the quality of the work they've done, or the parts they've used.

Searching websites such as eBay and Craigslist to see what the average selling prices are for the model you're considering will give you a ballpark idea. Of course, you will still need to do your own inspection.

A website called vintageairstream.com breaks vintage Airstreams into several categories to make it easier to get an idea on what the price should be for trailers in various conditions.

Vintageairstream.com classifies them as the following:

As-Found Condition: This trailer will require the most work. As-Found Condition may have many dents or punctures in the exterior skin, missing or broken vents and windows, bad electrical, and LP gas systems. A rotted subfloor will also be common. This trailer has not seen use in many years. It was likely left to rot in a field somewhere.

Average Condition: Is an older trailer that has very few or no dents and no punctures to the exterior skin. More than likely it is not polished. It should have all the original exterior vents covers, and working windows. Working appliances could be original, or properly replaced with newer models. There should also be a solid subfloor. Basically, the trailer should be in a working condition having seen regular use.

Restored Condition: This trailer will have been restored to original condition. Everything should work and look like it did when it was newer, and necessary updates for safety have been completed. In short, this trailer should be updated to have all systems working as original, but retain the original feeling of the trailer.

Renovated Condition: A renovated trailer is basically the same as the restored trailer where everything works. However, no requirement to keeping the trailer original was in mind. Newer technologies may be incorporated in plain view, which can include flat panel TV's, computers, and changed layouts. These trailers have been heavily altered to the owners taste and may not be something anyone else would enjoy.

Lets follow a 60's era Caravel through these steps to give you an idea of the costs involved. A Caravel in an As-Found Condition may be in the range of $2,000-$3,800. This same trailer ready to use in Average Condition would set you back $5,200−$8,900. Finally, the Restored Condition of this Caravel could run you somewhere between $12,900 and $17,800. Keep in mind that these are all examples from vintageairstream.com. Finding a properly restored Airstream available for sale would be a difficult task.

In my experience from producing the last seven years of the VAP, I believe the Restored Condition estimates to be quite low. I think that you should start by doubling their estimates.

When looking for a good restoration project trailer, I recommend looking for something in between the As-Found and Average Condition. The reason I say this is because you want to have a trailer with good aluminum skin, without punctures or large dents. On the flip side, you don't want to pay more because things are working that you don't want or need. Maybe the original refrigerator is working now, but you are likely going to need to replace it. The water heater might work for a while, like my Bowen, and then go out, so you'd need a new one. The point here is that you do not want to pay extra for things you won't need in your restoration.

Chapter Four

Trailer Inspections

Trailer Inspections

This is one of those 'Do as I say, not as I do moments'. I want to make sure that you always inspect the trailer before you buy it. Unfortunately, I had to inspect my Ambassador *after* I purchased it, which is certainly not the way to do it. This chapter will guide you on what to look for when inspecting these vintage beauties.

Knowing what you are getting into from the start will help set your expectations and restoration budget from the beginning. It's all about attitude. If you think you're getting a trailer that has been partially restored and won't require much in the way of repairs, you may be in for a big let down. You might be paying more than the trailer is worth. On the other hand, if you're going into this knowing that you will be gutting the entire trailer and rebuilding it from the ground up, then you can take every setback as an opportunity. This also gives you the edge to negotiate a fair starting price. That's what I did, and to be honest, that's the only way to do it.

The Semi-Monocoque Design

To properly inspect an Airstream you need to know how they are built, which is a topic that we discuss in depth in *Episode 16: Airstream Construction*.

Vintage Airstreams were built using a semi-monocoque or single-shell design that gives the Airstream its lightweight and strength. The semi-monocoque design of Airstreams is made up of three major components; the frame, subfloor, and aluminum shell. It is critical for the long-term viability of the trailer that all three be in top condition.

Frame: The frame is the metal chassis that the subfloor is affixed to. The Airstream frames have changed a lot over the years. The frames on the older trailers used a thinner gauge of steel then the newer models, which help make the vintage trailers lighter. Frame rust is common because of exposure to the elements over the decades. Water penetrates the trailer through missing rivets and cracks in the seams where it travels between the inner and outer shell making its way to the bellypan, where its saturates the insulation like a wet sponge. Over time, the frame rails and cross members can rust out, and will need to be replaced during the restoration. In severe cases, a complete frame replacement is necessary.

Airstream trailers have an enclosed underbelly that will limit your ability to fully inspect the frame. All that you have access to during your inspection are the exposed frame rails leaving the back of the trailer that the bumper is attached to, and the front of the trailer frame where the coupler is located. Be sure to look for rust-holes and cracked welds. Check that the frame is straight, especially near the front A-frame. Walk around the perimeter of the trailer, and look for tears in the shell near the floor level, as this could be a sign of broken frame outriggers.

Some trailer models have a rear trunk for storage in addition to the rear bumper. Take time to closely examine the rear frame rails that leave the back of the trailer that the bumper is attached to as these can show signs of rust holes or other damage. Look down at the rear of the trailer behind the bumper for places that water may have penetrated the trim work through missing sealant or dents in the trim. Behind this panel, beneath the floor level, is a rear cross member on the frame that is well known for being rusted out. While you are at the rear bumper, place your foot on it and push it down forcing the trailer to move up and down. Carefully watch the rear of the trailer body, and see that it follows the frame's up and down motion. If it doesn't, you have a good candidate for frame separation.

Frame separation occurs when the shell becomes disconnected from the subfloor and frame. The cause of the separation is because the bolts and screws that hold the shell to the frame have come loose, or have broken away from a rusted frame. If your trailer has this separation, you will need to repair it before it causes more damage.

The front of the trailer may have a metal plate on the inside of the front wall that helps hold the shell to the front of the frame. This plate sits on top of the frame directly below the front window. We talk in depth about this on *Episode 147: Plateless Airstreams*. The plate is not on every model trailer, but it is on most vintage units. You will see a number of rivet rows immediately behind where the propane tanks sit and you should make sure these rivets are in place and are not loose.

As I mentioned in the Search by Era chapter, there is a phenomenon called frame sag or tail droop. Tail droop is very common in the 70's era mostly affecting trailers over 25-feet or longer, where the frames started to bend just after the rear axles. The axle seemed to act as a fulcrum point for the frame sag. There was a factory repair using metal plates to strengthen the frame. If the model of trailer you are inspected is susceptible to tail-droop, be sure to check for the metal plate repair, or two bellypan patches near the axles where the repairs would have been made. If you intend to buy a trailer with tail-droop, it will need to be repaired.

All Airstream's have an enclosed underbelly that makes it difficult to fully inspect the frame. Experience has shown that some of the cross-members will need to be replaced, especially the rear one. If the frame looks good in general, I would not worry too much about it. They will all have some kind of issue that will need to be addressed.

The ideal way to examine the frame would be to remove sections of the bellypan to expose the frame for inspection. It's not likely the seller would allow this, so be prepared for the trailer to reveal more gremlins after you purchase it and begin your restoration.

Subfloor: The subfloor is the second main structural element in the trailer. During construction the subfloor is bolted to the frame, then an aluminum c-channel is bolted to the subfloor and frame. Finally, the shell is riveted to this c-channel. Now you can understand why a strong subfloor is vital, because it's holding the shell on. Like most vintage Airstreams, the Ambassador had its share of rotted subflooring. The last ten inches or so of plywood around the rear perimeter was rotted out, which needed to be replaced. I'd even venture to say that if you don't have a photo of yourself inside your trailer standing on the ground, you missed a restoration step!

Water is the root cause of damaged subfloors as it can find its way through cracks in the seams and enter the walls. The walls channel the water right to the edge of the subfloor and causes it to rot over the years. The edge of the subfloor is the most critical part, because that is where the shell is attached via the aluminum c-channel. This is why standing in the middle of an Airstream, and bouncing up and down to 'test the floor' is not an appropriate or adequate test.

Airstream experimented with different types of subfloor material. Plywood is the most prevalent and the most desired wood, as it seems to hold up the best. In later years, oriented strand board or OSB was used. Oriented strand board is manufactured using wood strips, wax, and adhesives. Experience has shown that OSB does not stand up very well against water and damages easily. Typically, the '80's and part of the 90's used OSB, then Airstream switched back to plywood for the subfloors.

For a short time Airstream experimented using a honeycomb synthetic subfloor in certain years of its Argosy line of trailers. It's really unknown as to why they stopped using it, perhaps it was due to cost considerations.

In *Episode 127: Look a SOB*, Colin talks about his favorite floor inspection tools. He likes to inspect floors with a flashlight and an icepick. The idea here is that you want to look as close to the edge of the floor as possible where it meets the shell. The best place will be in the cabinetry like the bathroom vanity and the kitchen cabinet. Take your flashlight and look in the back of a cabinet up against the wall. If there is carpet, peel back a small section and take the icepick and strike the wood floor with it. If the floor is in good shape, you'll only be able to put a small dimple in it. But if the pick goes into the wood, or in a really bad case, through it, you've found rot.

There will almost always be some amount of wood rot. Common places are under the vanity, under just about any window, and right at the entry door. In some cases you only need to replace the bad section, but you must replace it all the way out to the edge. Remember, the edge of the subfloor, through the frame, is what holds the shell on. If there is a great deal of wood rot, replacing the entire subfloor may make the most sense. Replacing the entire floor may not be something you want to deal with, so you might pass on a trailer with that much rot. Although, many home enthusiasts have repaired entire subfloors themselves, you can have a professional replace the subfloor. Once they have replaced it, you can take on the project from there.

Shell: The aluminum shell is the last in our trio of semi-monocoque components. The shell is the most resilient of the three. You can easily see it's condition from a visual inspection. The most important item to look for is damage to the endcaps. For some reason, the front and rear endcaps seem to have dents in them, with the rear endcaps having very large dents. I suspect these dents are from backing into trees or over hangs. Always look up when backing a trailer! Vintage Airstream endcaps can be very difficult to repair, however, there are some dent pullers like the Ding King that have limited success. Most panels in the endcaps are stretch-formed at the factory, and cannot be rebuilt easily in a repair shop. The best option, if you find yourself in this dilemma, is to locate a wrecked Airstream and use its panels for the repair. In *Episode 80: Body Works* we talk a great deal about dents and how to repair them, realizing that sometimes you'll have to learn to live with them. We call them beauty marks!

While you're inspecting the shell you want to look for gouges, scratches, and dings of all sorts, because these imperfections have a way of revealing themselves once a trailer is polished. There are also instances where the aluminum can corrode and become weaker and thinner than the panels around it. The corroded panel will need to be replaced. You won't really know this until you have the inside walls off and can inspect the interior side of the panel. From my experience this is not very common since we have not heard many complaints about it on the program.

For the most part, you want the shell to be as dent free as possible. As long as you don't see a lot of corrosion on your inspection, you're likely to be fine. Remember, these trailers are thirty, forty, or even fifty years old. There will be imperfections in the skin. It's best to learn to live with the smaller beauty marks. They add character.

They ALL Leak

One of the long time running jokes on the show over the last seven years has been, 'They all leak.'   It's quite the misconception that Airstreams don't leak. When I was searching for my first Airstream the sellers would tell me, "All you need to know about Airstreams is they don't leak!" I'm here to tell you they *do* leak. Not only do they leak, but ALL OF THEM LEAK, including the new ones.

The reason owners have this misconception is because of the way Airstreams are built. The trailer is built with a double aluminum shell with about 1-$\frac{1}{2}$ inches of space between the walls. When the exterior shell leaks due to missing rivets or cracks in the sealant, water runs inside the trailer. In many cases the water stays between the outer shell and the interior shell where it accesses the subfloor and causes damage. The owner never sees water dripping inside the trailer and assumes they never leak.

It could very well be that Airstream trailers leak less than SOB's (Some Other Brand trailer). When Airstreams do leak they *handle* it much better, because the only wood in an Airstream is the subfloor, so there really isn't any wall support damage. In an SOB with wood framing, the damage can be substantial.

Leaks often occur on the aluminum seams where the sheets overlap one another. When the trailers are built they are protected on the inside with a coating on the seam that can fail over time and allow water leaks. In addition, some trailer models have what is called a belly wrap, which is formed by connecting aluminum from the bellypan under the trailer to the sides. The joint where the belly wrap meets the side of the trailer is covered by trim work. Leaks in the trim can allow water to funnel right into the belly through cracks in the sealant.

Loose or broken windows, missing vents, and dents can affect the trailers resistance to the elements. All of these items will need to be addressed during the restoration phase and will be a constant maintenance issue for your trailer.

Before we leave this subject, we often hear the question of whether or not to use tarps to cover your Airstream. This can actually lead to scratches on the aluminum surface, because as the wind blows the tarp against the trailer skin it acts like coarse sandpaper. We recommend keeping your trailer watertight with the proper sealants, and by replacing missing rivets and screws during yearly maintenance. It's beneficial to store your trailer indoors, but that's not always practical.

Appliances

Common appliances in a vintage Airstream will be a refrigerator, water heater, furnace, and an oven or stovetop. If you are really interested that these items work, I would let the seller know that you intend to inspect them. Whatever you do, don't take their word for it. Test everything yourself.

Of course, depending on your restoration goal, it might not make any sense to inspect them at all. You don't want to give them any unnecessary value if you intend to replace them anyway, but you should think about using their condition as a bargaining opportunity. If you want to keep things original for your restoration, take the time to check them carefully as working appliances, that are vintage, will be hard to find and even harder to keep running. I didn't really care about the appliances in the Ambassador, since I was planning on installing new ones anyway.

Proper RV refrigerators run on propane and sometimes 110-VAC. These mobile refrigerators work through absorption and can take as much as 12 hours to cool down. I would recommend having the seller turn the refrigerator on in gas mode the night before you want to inspect it, which gives you the added benefit of testing the propane system as well as the refrigerator. Once the refrigerator has been on for 8–12 hours, check that the interior freezer and refrigerator compartments are cold. The real secret to keeping the refrigerator temperatures down are good soft playable gaskets that seal the door completely, so be sure to look them over carefully during your inspection. While you are examining the refrigerator, check that the inside is free of cracks. There are ways to fix these cracks and gaskets if the refrigerator is a vintage one that you want to keep for your restoration.

RV refrigerators work by cycling ammonia through the rear absorber coils of the unit. If the ammonia leaks, there will be residue on the coils. There should be an access hatch on the outside of the trailer to inspect the back of the refrigerator. Check the back carefully for green or white residue on the coils, if you see it, the fridge is shot because the residue is leaked ammonia. You can have the cooling unit replaced by a specialized shop. My understanding is that the results are not very good, because there are issues creating the original thermal bond between the cooling unit and the refrigeration box. Many times this bond fails, and you loose proper thermal transfer. In my opinion, you're better off installing a modern refrigerator.

Be on the look out for standard apartment style 110-VAC only replacement refrigerators. It's very common for sellers to replace a failed RV refrigerator with a small apartment model, which are not appropriate for camping or boondocking without hookups. The reason sellers will put a small standard refrigerator in the trailer is because they are inexpensive. An apartment style refrigerator can be purchased for around $100 when a RV propane operated refrigerator will start at around $600. The whole point of a travel trailer is to be mobile, and an apartment style refrigerator will only work when connected to shore power. So unless you're going to park your trailer and never move it, put a proper propane refrigerator on your restoration todo list.

Next up is the water heater. You can only test the water heater if the plumbing system is working, as the water heater must be full of water before heating it. By testing the water heater you'll be pressurizing the water system too, which will give you the opportunity to check for leaks. To get started, have the seller connect a water hose to the city water inlet, which will pressurize the water system and allow you to check for leaks. Plumbing in an Airstream is usually accessible behind cabinets or under beds, so it should not be too difficult to examine the system. Have the seller light the water heater and give you some instruction on how to do it. You should expect the water to heat up in about 20−30 minutes. If the water heater is a pilot light only model, the burner should cut back to only the pilot flame after it reaches temperature. Then you can check for hot water at the hot water taps. Have a look at as much plumbing as possible, and look for water leaks in the pipes and fixtures. Original plumbing will be copper piping. Replacement plumbing can be copper or a popular DIY alternative called PEX. Disconnect the city water inlet and repeat the test using the on-demand water pump and fresh water tank.

On the VAP we do not think too highly of vintage furnaces. This is one area that you do not want to gamble with. It's one thing to risk losing hot water or having a warm refrigerator while camping. It's safety hazard to use a faulty furnace. Furnaces use a combustion chamber to burn gas and blow the heated air into the trailer for warmth. Overtime, these combustion chambers can rust and develop cracks, which allow carbon monoxide into the trailer. There are also gaskets and rubber tubes that transport air in and out of the trailer, and into the combustion chamber. These gaskets and tubes can get brittle overtime and cause problems as well. We are talking about issues related to age, not use. It's irrelevant that the furnace has not been used and looks new. For these safety reasons, we do not recommend using or rebuilding furnaces. If the furnace is more than 5 years old, I would highly recommend replacing it. Even if it is new, have it inspected by a professional, and *always* have a carbon monoxide detector in your trailer. In addition, we recommend keeping a window cracked open when camping. You probably guessed by now, that the furnace in the Ambassador was immediately trashed!

Stovetops and ovens can be tested fairly easily on inspection if the gas system works. For the most part, the oven will probably look pretty new, because not many people bake while camping. It's been a trend lately to leave out the oven for more cabinet space during a restoration. If you're trying to stay to the original time period, consider keeping it. Original ovens tend to add a lot of style to a vintage restoration. Most of the time, a good cleaning is all they need. Keep in mind, like the rest of the appliances, these are gas operated and deserve respect. Have a professional check them over if in doubt. I decided to get rid of the oven in the Ambassador, and replaced it with a stovetop and a convection microwave.

Axles

It's no secret, if you've ever listened to the show, that if the trailer has original axles they're bad. You might ask, "Why is that?" Let me tell you.

Before 1961 Airstream used leaf spring axles, which were common for trailers of the time and are still used today. These axles will need to be inspected for rust, missing parts, and may need to have the springs repaired.

According to Airstream history, the international caravans in the '50's were extremely rough on leaf spring axles. Although they were easy to repair, they were a major cause of breakdowns. To tackle this problem, Airstream introduced the Dura-Torque torsion axle beginning in 1961.

The Dura-Torque axle uses a special construction technique that allows rubber rods inside the axle to absorb road impacts. Another feature of the Dura-Torque axle, is that it allows for independent suspension, which really helps keep the trailer from taking on the full shock of the road. Dura-Torque axles have less individual parts to go bad when compared to leaf spring axles. This was a big improvement, which is why they became standard starting in 1961.

Even though torsion axles were a big improvement, they do have their own issues. Over the years, torsion axles sag due to rubber deteriorating and don't provide any suspension. Worse than that, they can actually hit their metal travel limits and give an abrupt jolt to the trailer when under tow. Experience has shown that 99% of these axles are bad, and will require replacement during the restoration. That's just my nice way of saying that you'll need new axles.

The Ambassador is a 1960 model, so it had leaf spring axles. If it were a 1961, it would have had worn out Dura-Torque axles. Either way I would have replaced them. The leaf springs were fine enough to get me back across country, but my ultimate goal was to put new torsion axles on the trailer. I don't care for the low ride height the original leaf spring axles give, so ordering new axles allowed me the opportunity to change it. This is an advantage of doing a custom restoration.

I could have had the springs on the original axles rebuilt and generally restored them, but if torsion axles were good enough for Airstream to change over in 1961, who am I to argue!

Missing Rivets

When you inspect your trailer's skin walk around it and keep an eye on the rivet lines. You are looking for missing, uneven, or improper rivets. While a missing rivet can mean a leak, uneven or oddly placed rivets could mean a repair has been made. Sellers have been known to hide accident damage by placing new sheets of aluminum directly over the damaged area and riveting it on. In some cases, you may see a double row of rivets. This is an improper repair, and it could be hiding structural damage.

Airstream used bucked rivets when they built the trailer. Bucked rivets will have a smooth rounded finish. Installation requires one person outside with a rivet gun, and another inside the trailer with a bucking bar. Bucked rivets are stronger than pop rivets that some Saturday mechanics use when making alterations or repairs. These are not strong enough for panel repairs, and they prone to leak so keep an eye out for them.

In general, one or two missing rivets is nothing to be overly concerned about. If the number adds up, it could be sign of a major structural problem. Unless you are prepared to dig in deep, it may be best to pass.

Brakes and Tires

Tires and brakes are nothing to be lax about. These need to be in good shape for your tow home. If a tire blows due to rot, which you can't always see, it can do some extensive damage to the trailer. Look for small cracks in the sidewall and between the tire treads. If you see any sign of rot, do not use the tires.

Trailer tires only last about five years regardless of how they look. They don't move as often as a car tire, so they often rot quicker from the inside out. When tires are made, the manufacturer puts a Tire Identification Number on the sidewall. This identification number indicates the date the tire was made. Learn how to read the code so you can have a good idea on the tire's age.

Don't expect to have usable tires on the trailer you're inspecting. Not only will you need to replace the tires as part of your restoration, you will need them for the 'Recovery Mission'.

Exterior Lights

You'll need working lights on the trailer when towing it home. Proper lighting is a safety factor, besides you don't want to get a ticket. You can go about this one of two ways. You can do what I did and take some time with the trailer trying to repair the original lighting, or you can do what the Panel Pro's recommend, which is to bring a set of temporary trailer lights. Temporary lights have magnetic bases that attach to the trailer bumper. The wires from the lights run the distance of the trailer on the outside, and plug into the vehicle's towing package plug. Bring some aluminum tape to tape the wires along the side of the trailer. Never use duct tape, because it leaves a very sticky residue that's hard to remove.

One things for certain, *always* make sure the lights work before leaving!

What About Dents?

The first thing I do when inspecting a trailer is walk around it examining the skin. It's an obvious first step, but be sure to take your time and engage your mind in what your doing.

As you look at your trailer, keep an eye out for dents and tears from loose outriggers that break free from the frame. Loose outriggers can rip through the shell, creating cracks or bulges around the lower exterior walls. A dent in any panel is always a bad thing to have to deal with, and the worst dents are those found in either the front or rear endcap. If the endcap is a 13 panel, those sections can be recreated as they are cut from flat stock. Anything less than 13 panels, the pieces are stretch-formed at the factory and cannot be replicated easily. Most of the time you will be looking for a totaled trailer with an intact endcap that you can use parts from. It will be a very costly and labor-intensive endeavor to repair it. A dent can often be pulled out, but usually the aluminum stretches so the area will look a *little* off. If you can live with it, so can I.

A lot of times the rear bumpers will be bent, most likely from backing into a tree or some such obstruction. I wonder if it's the same guy who puts the dents in the rear endcaps. If the bumper is welded on, it will have to be cut or ground off the trailer and straightened.   There are metal shops that can handle a job like this.

It's always best to find a shell with the least amount of damage as possible. If you find too many problems with your prospective trailer, it may be best to pass on it and wait for the next one.

Condition of Skin

It is common for Airstream trailers to have what Rob calls, 'Airstream pattern baldness'. Many Airstreams had clearcoat sprayed on them at the factory to keep the aluminum looking nice and shiny, and to protect against oxidation. Over the years, the sun beats down on the coating and weakens it, and it starts to peel from the top of the trailer working its way down. The Ambassador had this problem too. I really don't recommend trying to restore the clearcoat, because they always fail given enough exposure to UV rays. In my opinion, the repair for this is also the first step necessary to polishing the trailer. You have to use a chemical stripper to remove the remaining clearcoat. It's vital to any kind of polish job that all of the clearcoat be removed.

Peeling clearcoat allows oxygen and water under the coating and sometimes causes a special kind of corrosion called filiform, which looks like very tiny white worms under the remaining clearcoat. This corrosion is very difficult to remove during the polishing phase of your restoration. It is possible, but it will take some extra effort.

Other types of corrosion on the aluminum may be so bad that you will have to replace the panel. A lot of times you won't find it until you start polishing your trailer. What you may see is a surface that looks uneven when compared to other parts of the trailer. What is happening is the aluminum has corroded and thinned over time. If it's bad enough, the panel will need to be replaced. I have one area on the Ambassador that is badly pitted from corrosion. Lucky for me it's not yet weak enough that I need to do anything about it. Still, it does not polish up as nice as the rest of the trailer.

Another issue you might see is small dents from rocks being kicked up at the front of the trailer. You may find scratches and scrapes of all kinds, some of which can be polished away, but a lot will have to be lived with and accepted. A polished trailer will bring out all these imperfections. It's best to learn to live with them.

Chapter Five

Recovery Mission

At the 24-hour Truck and Tire shop.

Buying Our Airstream

Winning bid:	**US $3,377.88**
	Get low monthly payments
Ended:	**Jun-03-06 19:14:36 PDT**
Shipping:	Buyer responsible for vehicle pick-up or shipping. Vehicle shipping quote is available.
Sells to:	Worldwide
Item location:	Carey, Ohio, United States
History:	31 bids
Winning bidder:	ME ! (90 ★)
You can also:	Email to a friend	Sell one like this

Final eBay bid.

It was the evening of June 3, 2006 when Debra was doing some eBay searching for vintage Airstreams. She called me up to the office to show me an auction for a 28-foot trailer. I looked it over, but I wasn't too sure if we should do it. I noticed the bid activity was pretty high, so we'd have some competition. That's never a good thing in an auction.

The ad said the trailer was in good condition, and the pictures looked good. The outside shell was straight, and the layout was nice, but what drew Debra to this trailer was the photo of the dinette that showed a nice wrap-around couch with pretty wall sconces and flowers on the wall. In addition, the ad clearly stated it slept six. She knew we were looking to sleep at least five. After looking at trailer ads endlessly for weeks, this seemed to be one of the better trailers available that matched our needs.

I saw a few dents in the belly wrap from the photos of the street side, but nothing that concerned me too much. The layout looked pretty good, and was fairly close to what we had in our Safari, which was fine, because there were a lot of things we liked about the Safari's layout. The living area was up front and blended into the kitchen. In the middle of the trailer was a set of twin beds, which is great, because we really like having beds that are always available for a quick nap. Some times you need to convert a couch or dining table to form a bed, so this was an advantage to us.

Heading on to the rear of the trailer revealed a large bathroom with two closets, a vanity, toilet, and a large bathtub. I was really impressed with how large the bathroom is in this trailer. In our old Safari we had to constantly shift people around in order to gain any kind of privacy. The Ambassador's bathroom is large enough that you can go inside, close the door, shower, and get dressed without having to disturb anyone else.

Everything looked great on this trailer, but there was a small problem. The trailer was in Carey, OH and we're in northern California, 2400 miles away. It would be quite the trip just to pick it up. Oh yeah, there was one more little issue. The eBay auction was ending in just *one* hour!

I decided that I needed some help! I needed a pro! I wanted to talk to one of the Panel of Pro's from my show and get some advice. I made a frantic call to Rob, but he didn't answer! I got his voicemail! My next call was to Colin, and after several rings, seemingly forever, he *finally* answered. As it tuned out, Colin and Rob were attending a rally together. I started telling Colin about the trailer in the auction to get some advice on what I should do. Colin kept saying it sounded good to him. He had a certain dismissive nature when I pointed out if a repair could be made or not. Colin would say, "Anything can be done." Sure, that's easy for him to say, he's a pro *and* 3000 miles away!

I was really hoping Colin would tell me to skip it. Maybe the trailer was too far-gone, or at least too far away. I'm sure it was too risky, too much of an unknown. I knew it had to be *too* something, and I wanted him to tell me why I shouldn't buy it. He never did.

In the last minute of the auction, I made my one and only bid for $3,377.88. Colin, Rob, and I counted down the last 60 seconds together over the phone. I think by now they were drawing a small crowd around them at the rally, because when I announced that I had *won* it, I heard laughter and cheering from 3000 miles away. The sound of laughter was a little unsettling. I thought to myself, "What have I done? ...Again."

Prepping for the Pickup

Once you have found your trailer you have to switch modes. You have to go from searching for a trailer to thinking about how to bring it home. On the show we refer to this as the 'Recovery Mission'. That's in fact what they are, a mission. You never know what you're going to find until you get there, so you have to prepare for any contingency. If you fail to plan, then you plan to fail. You've heard that before, but it's true, especially when dealing with vintage trailers. These old trailers can be stuck in mud, have a frozen tongue jack, or rotted tires. The lights may not work, and the brakes could be frozen. There will be any number of obstacles for you to overcome.

In *Episode 15: Bringing It Home*, we talk about many things you need to consider when you go to pick up your trailer. In episodes 35 and 36 we talk about The Mission. Rob was picking up a vintage Airstream for a friend and all kinds of craziness ensued. It's a fun listen, as it starts off with Rob showing up at night to pick up the trailer, and the key for it was 1000 miles away. It ended with Rob and his family stuck on the side of the road days later. The trailer was missing a wheel, and his young son covered in wheel bearing grease! Colin and Rob advised me to listen to *Episode 15: Bringing it Home* before I left town. I highly recommend you take their advice.

I called the seller, Joe, in advance to let him know my plans to pick up the trailer. I wanted to make sure I had Joe's cell phone number, and that he would be available the day we pulled into town. Now that Joe was squared away, it was time to load up with the recovery supplies.

My 1960 trailer had a 2" coupler, which is different then my Safari, which had a 2 5/16". I needed to bring a 2" ball with me along with the tools to change it. You should always verify the size of the trailer's hitch with the seller before you head out.

Always assume the tires are shot. I purchased some tires locally and brought them with me. As you'll find out later, this turned out to be a great idea.

Bring a rope.   Over the many years of the VAP we talk repeatedly about sprung entry doors. A sprung door is one that has flown open while traveling down the highway and slammed into the side of the trailer. Besides damaging the trailer, it knocks the curve right out of the door, so it never seals right when closed.   Even worse, the door can fly off the trailer and land on the freeway somewhere, which is a good way to lose a door. On a 'Recovery Mission', we always recommend bringing a rope to tie the door closed. Yes, it looks pretty lame, but it beats losing your door! On *Episode 8: Mystery Guest Revealed!*, we describe a wooden doohickey that can be built to keep a door from opening. It only works on certain models, but you might as well give that a listen. I ended up using a rope even though I didn't like to, but it wasn't worth the risk. I had a deadbolt installed before the trip home.   That's the permanent fix.

Aluminum tape was next on my list. A lot of people might substitute duct tape, but I wouldn't recommend it, as duct tape will leave a lot of residue behind on the aluminum skin. If the tape is left on the trailer's skin long enough, it breaks down and becomes a real mess when trying to remove it. Always bring aluminum tape.

New safety chains are a must have. Safety chains keep the trailer from running free from the tow vehicle in the event of a hitch failure. Obviously, you don't know the condition of these chains when you leave your house, so bring some chains and locking links with you. On one of Rob's recovery missions, he had a worn out coupler that caused the trailer to jump right off the hitch. The only thing that saved him was the safety chain! Remember to crisscross the chains under the coupler when connecting to your tow vehicle. The X you form with the crossed chains is what catches and holds the trailer tongue if it jumps off the ball. I had new chains installed before my tow home.

A floor jack is a nice thing to bring. I sure wish that I had one after we arrived. You'll learn what happened to me a little later.

Bring some temporary tow lights. It is critical to have operating trailer lights before you take to the road. You need to have working running lights, blinkers, and of course, brake lights before you head home.

Bring a basic set of hand tools like wrenches, sockets, pliers, hammers, and electrical tape. Just throw your toolbox in your vehicle before you head out. It's better to have something and not need it then need it, than need it and not have it.

2400 Miles

My personal 'Recovery Mission' was a major one for me, mostly because of the distance. The trailer that we won on eBay was 2400 miles from our home, and it was quite the journey just to get to it. Let alone what I found once we made it there. At first my wife wanted to make a vacation out of it by going with me and bringing the kids along. I didn't think this type of trip was going to be of family vacation quality, as I knew that the trailer wouldn't be family friendly. There would be no plumbing, refrigeration, or heating. It would basically be an aluminum tent, and a dirty one at that. Bringing the wife and kids would give them a bad impression of the trailer for sure. In addition, we'd also need to stop at hotels every night, and my goal was to get there and back as cheap as possible. This meant driving late into the night, and sleeping in the trailer.

Debra didn't want me to drive that distance alone, so like the El Paso trip, I enlisted the help of my dad. Dad's always up for an adventure, at least that's the impression he gives, and we love him for it!

Less than a week after winning the Airstream on eBay, we set out across country. It was just a couple of men, a road, and a mission. Life was good. We'd sleep in the truck at rest stops; eat on the road, driving for endless hour after hour. Sounds glamorous, like the ultimate road trip adventure. I'm sure it would have been, if we were 20. However, sleeping in the truck was uncomfortable, and driving endlessly without stopping isn't all that glamorous. It's tiresome.

We did enjoy our time together. We discussed just about everything in the world. That's a good thing to do with your family any time, but a road trip with dad, made it worth the time. No life distractions, just one on one time with pops. Trailering is about family time together. What better way to start, then on a 'Recovery Mission' together?

Inspecting the Ambassador

After four days of driving, Dad and I pulled into Carey, OH on a Sunday afternoon. My dad and I met with Joe behind his store where the trailer was parked. One of the first things I did was walk around the trailer, and start my exterior inspection. I was shocked to see large rust holes on the frame rails leaving the rear of the trailer. To be honest, I started freaking out. I called Colin, and I'm sure he could tell I was upset, as I told him about the frame rails being rusted with gaping holes! He said something like, "Yep, we see that a lot, it can be repaired." That comment was not very comforting since I'm not a welder. Just a reminder, the eBay photos looked great. There wasn't any photos of rusted out frames, which would have kept me from bidding on it in the first place.

Luckily, the Ambassador had fairly good skin all the way around it, which I *could* see in the eBay photos before we left. I looked around outside, and checked the panels for odd rivet lines or missing rivets. Everything checked out fine in that area.

I noticed a missing Astrodome vent cover that should have been on the roof. In it's place was a garbage can lid held on with a brick. Astrodome is Airstream's name for the large vent cover in the living room area of the trailer. It's very common for the Astrodome to be missing since they are made of fiberglass and over the years the sun beats down on them, causing them to get brittle and fall apart. Since we were heading back across country, I had to tape plastic over the open hole using my aluminum tape. Again, there were no photos of the missing vent on eBay.

Front dinette as found, missing table. Fabric thumbtacked to a wood frame.

As I said, the photos on the auction are what drew Debra to our particular trailer. One photo showed the front of the inside of the trailer with a nice wrap around couch in a Route 66 theme with maroon curtains, pretty sconces, and flowers on the wall.   As expected, what I found was very different from the pictures. The couch was nothing more than a 2x4 wood frame screwed to the floor that the owner literally thumb tacked maroon colored cloth to it trying to make it look nice. The wall sconces were house types barely attached to the wall, and totally useless in a travel trailer. I could have raised a fuss over this obvious sham, but I did come over 2000 miles to pick up this trailer. I knew that I was going to be doing a full restoration, so I didn't make an issue over it.

It's no surprise that the appliances had issues. The Ambassador had a small apartment style AC only refrigerator in it. I didn't really care about the refrigerator because I was going to replace it. The eBay auction said the refrigerator worked, and after testing, it didn't. I was able to get Joe to reduce the price by $50.

The water heater was another surprise. The previous owner installed a small electric-only household water heater in it. It's really interesting what owners do to avoid doing proper RV repairs. The electric water heater was one more thing for me to haul back to California just to throw away. I don't think Joe did these repairs, because I got the impression he had recently purchased the trailer from a young lady. I'm not sure what Joe intended to do with the trailer, but of course, he turned around and flipped it on eBay.

The fresh water tank was missing. It should have been up front under the couch, but all that was left was the original fill tube. The tank would have been an aluminum cylinder capable of being pressurized. At least the original toilet was there. The only problem was that it was broken. All of this did not concern me that much, because I knew I would be replacing all of it during my restoration.

Even after seeing all of this, I was still going to buy the trailer. Unfortunately, the trailer jack was frozen in the up position. We had to find a way to raise the tongue high enough to get it on my truck's hitch. I wish that I had brought a floor jack, because my truck's jack was not big enough to raise the tongue where we needed it. I remember we had to keep stacking wood blocks to get it high enough. Once we backed the truck up to the trailer, we had to kick the blocks out and let the tongue drop onto the ball of the hitch. Not recommended by the way!

Keep in mind that these trailers are thirty, forty, and even fifty years old. There will be problems, and you will find things on your inspection that the owner neglected to mention. It's all part of the experience. When I saw my trailer in person, after driving 2400 miles, even I was a little taken back. It's hard to drive that far and walk away, but if there were a great deal of damage, like it was in an accident or major structural problems, it would still be the smart thing to do. What I saw was the same things you'll see, and as Colin would say, "It can all be fixed".

With my experience from doing the VAP, I expected much of what I encountered. Since you're reading this book, you'll know what to expect too, as my experiences are fairly common.

Probably the biggest mistake I made is that I brought a cashiers check for the full purchase price. What I should have done is brought the cashiers check made out for $500 less than the total and brought the rest in cash. This would have provided me with some wiggle room on the final price. Just because the eBay auction closed at a certain amount, doesn't mean you can't adjust it if the item was not presented accurately.

Getting it Roadworthy

To get the Ambassador roadworthy I needed to get the lights working, tires ready, and secure the windows and vents. I spent some time cleaning the 7-way plug on the trailers umbilical cable trying to get the lights to work on my trailer. I ended up using a nail file, small flat head screwdriver, and contact cleaner to clean and bend the contacts back into working order. Then I had to pull some light covers off the trailer and clean the bulb sockets and swap lamps around until I got everything working. It probably took longer that it should have, which is why the Pros don't bother with it.

Next I took the aluminum tape and taped every window closed. I didn't care if the operators and locks worked or not, they got taped shut. While I was at it, I climbed on the roof so that I could tape the vents closed, because I didn't want anything flying off down the highway.

On the inside I made sure that everything that could be closed was, like the refrigerator door, drawers, and cabinet doors. Anything big or heavy got stowed on the floor. One thing that I should have done was tape the light covers on, because I ended up having a glass cover from one of the ceiling fixtures fall off during the first 50 miles; getting shattered glass everywhere. The cover was one of those hard to find parts that took me about three years to get a replacement.

After closing the door to the trailer, out came the nylon rope. I tied the door closed by looping around the door handle and running it up to the tongue. This would keep the door from flying open until I could get a deadbolt installed.

The last thing we did was use dad's portable air compressor to pump some air in the tires. That took lot of time since the little 12-VDC compressor had to cool for 10 minutes for every 5 minutes of pumping. I don't remember how much air we ended up getting in those tires, but it wasn't much. It did do the job though, and we were thankful to have that little compressor.

We pulled away from Carey, OH at the blistering speed of 30 mph. Cars and trucks were passing us on that two-lane road. I'm sure they were mumbling something about crazy California drivers. At one point we had to pull over, because I notice the entrance step opened up, which would become a regular occurrence. I'd learn later, during the restoration, that it was caused by a loose outrigger that supported the step.

We were desperate to get the new tires I had brought with us on the trailer. We looked and looked and couldn't find a tire shop open. There wasn't even a gas station that could help us. After an hour of driving, we happened to see a 24-hour truck and tire shop. This was a lucky find for us, but the garage was obviously setup for servicing big rigs, not vintage trailers. All I cared about is that they were open on a Sunday. We went in to ask them if they could replace my trailer tires they said "Sure, if you have them". They didn't carry tires that small! So bringing the tires with me paid off huge. The shop replaced my tires and checked the brakes. By the time we left there we had new tires, properly inflated, with working brakes and lights, we were in fat city! We could even go the speed limit!

Aluminum Tent

Camping at the Mother Ship.

Home at the Mother Ship. That's what we call the Airstream factory on the show. The factory is in Ohio and so were we. I thought we might as well stop for a visit. Hey, I'm an Airstreamer now after all, I might as well bring the trailer back to where it had been built 46 years earlier. The factory is in Jackson Center, which was only an hour and a half from where we picked up the Ambassador.

Airstream has a nice little campground for visitors called the Terraport. If you are getting work done on your trailer, you get to stay there for free. We made it to the factory that night, and since we had the trailer with us, we were going to make use of it and sleep in it; right at the Airstream factory campground. Is there any better place to stay the first night in a new Airstream?

I didn't know what worked on the trailer, so of course I wouldn't be using any gas-operated appliances or plumbing. All I hoped for was that the electrical system would give us light, so I took a chance and plugged the trailer into shore power. Low and behold, there was light! My Ambassador is the International model that has 110-VAC lighting. Lucky for us it still worked!

On the show, we call trailers that don't have much in the way of amenities working, aluminum tents. We usually talk about this on the flip side after the restoration build up has started, but hey, we were a long way from home, so we stayed in our aluminum tent!

Waiting for service at the Terraport.

The next day at the factory I decided to have the Airstream shop take care of a couple of issues for me. The first was to upgrade my original 2" coupler to a new 2-5/16". Technically, it wasn't necessary to replace the coupler, but I wanted to have a working tongue jack for the drive home. I was worried something might happen, and I wanted to be able to disconnect the trailer if I needed to. I also hated having to rope the door closed. Man that looks tacky. So I had the factory install a deadbolt. They had an old-timer there who had installed them on vintage units before, so he worked on mine, installing our deadbolt. The funny part about that was the factory didn't have any deadbolts. I had to run to a local home improvement store and pick one up for them. Hey, did they charge me for that?

Standing next to Wally Byam's gold anodized Airstream.

While they were working on the trailer dad and I decided to take the factory tour, which starts at 2pm each day. They walk you through all of the different steps of trailer construction. We found it very interesting and recommend it if you are ever in the area, stop by the factory. It's worth a visit. Outside the factory Airstream parks some of the special vintage trailers from their past. One really unique trailer is Wally's gold anodized Airstream, and I was able to have my picture taken next to it. I know, kind of geeky, but not if you're an Airstreamer. You know that you would do it too if you could.

The factory finished up the work on our trailer right at closing time that night, so we hooked up our aluminum tent and set out for home. We used our trailer a few nights on the way staying in rest stops, and we used a hotel to freshen up at least once. Dad and I made it back in one piece, and the trailer did to. Thanks dad!

Overnight at a rest stop in our aluminum tent on the way home.

Chapter Six

The Restoration

Restoration Planning

Now that you've returned from your 'Recovery Mission' with your vintage trailer, you'll need to gear up for the restoration. Planning is the key to success. I hope when you were looking for your vintage Airstream that you took my advice and visited as many as you could in person. Perhaps you were able to attend an open house at a rally, which will really benefit you now as it should have given you some ideas about what you want in a trailer. Having a design before you start the work is extremely beneficial, because the more you can plan ahead, the less re-work you'll have to do. Try to envision that your restoration is complete, and you're already using your restored Airstream.

Debra chose our Ambassador based on the fact that the ad said it would sleep six. Even though the ad was much over-hyped, one of the design goals was to make sure that it would sleep the five people in our family.

I knew that I wanted to add a grey water tank since the trailer didn't have one, and the grey water would drain right on the ground. This was typical of '60s trailers. With this in mind, the design needed to make necessary accommodations for a new grey tank.

One of the reasons I wanted a vintage Airstream was because of it's low weight, and I didn't want to change that by dramatically altering the trailer. I intentionally chose lightweight materials and designs throughout the restoration.

I also wanted to increase ride height of the trailer, because I don't like the original 'low-rider' look that the leaf spring axles provide. Knowing this up front provided me with the opportunity to make modifications that would increase the ground clearance when I replaced the axles.

I wanted to install a couple of flat panel TV's as part of my restoration. I built the cabinetry with heavy-duty support to hold TV wall mounts along with the necessary wiring.

This just scratches the surface as far as planning goes, but it should give you an idea of the types of things you should consider when designing your restoration. You'll need to come up with your goals before you start any work on your trailer, as a lot of important decisions need to be made prior to tearing into it. Hopefully, reading this book will give you some ideas you had not considered that can be used in your restoration.

Types of Restorations

In *Episode 12: Restoration and Refurbishment* Rob, Colin, and I talk with the Vintage Airstream Club historian, Fred Caldwell, about the different ways to restore an Airstream. We covered the following:

Preservation is when you make every effort to keep a trailer the way you found it. If the trailer is a good representation of a vintage model that has not be modified, preserving the trailer is a good choice. These trailers are getting harder and harder to find.

Restoration is the most difficult task to undertake. Restoration is rebuilding the trailer to the way it rolled off the factory floor. You can use magazines and catalogs to get a feel for how the trailer looked. You can't let any modern technologies be seen.

Refurbishment is rebuilding the trailer much in the same way as a restoration, but not being overly critical about having to maintain the exact vintage appliances or furnishings. In a refurbishment, you have more leeway than a restoration.

Modernization is when you make the trailer into something you like without worrying about the past. You may include design concepts from your vintage era like using lightweight materials and layouts, but you maintain the freedom to move things to your liking. Modern amenities and high tech solutions can be utilized in plain view such as flat panel TVs and computers; as opposed to having to hide them in a refurbishment.

I decided to modernize the Ambassador. I really enjoy high tech gadgetry, and prefer new modern appliances. I didn't want my hands tied by staying true to a restoration. What you decide is a personal choice, but I would guess that most trailers would be somewhere between a refurbishment and modernization.

Common Problems

Over the years of producing theVAP we've probably heard all of the issues that will come up in a vintage restoration. From floor rot to filiform corrosion, we've heard it all. Here are some of the common problems that most vintage trailers will have; you should expect to find them your restoration.

There's no doubt that you've found floor rot during your inspection. Most of the time the last several feet of subfloor will need to be replaced, which you can do with the shell on without much difficulty. If you find subfloor rot in several areas like the rear of the trailer, under the front window, and by the door, you might consider replacing the entire floor. The best way to do this is with a complete shell-off floor replacement, which is more common than you might think. A shell-off floor replacement is exactly what it sounds like. You completely remove the shell from the frame to have open access for the subfloor replacement. Replacing the entire floor gives easier access for frame repairs, although it might be best to have this work performed by a professional.

In addition to floor rot, the rear frame cross member and many outriggers will typically be rotted and rusted through. Outriggers are frame members that extend from the main rails to support the subfloor. They often fail and break loose, especially the ones near entrance step. Much of this can be repaired from below with the bellypan removed. Even the mighty Ambassador had these issues.

For some reason there is a myth going around that Airstreams don't leak. Like we say on the show, "They ALL leak", and yours will too. You'll find that seams, trim, lights, and vents are all sources of leaks. In most cases you will not be able to see the leak, as it usually occurs between the inner and outer aluminum skins. A regular part of your maintenance will be to make sure there is sealant on all the seams and skin penetrations.

If you have a trailer before 1961, you will have leaf spring axles, and they will need to be checked for safety and proper operation. Starting in 1961, Airstream switched to torsion axles with a rubber rod suspension that will have deteriorated by now. You can count on replacing both the torsion axles and tires.

It's nearly a guarantee that the plumbing system will need to be replaced since the original plumbing was copper pipe, and will almost always have a problem with leaks. Over the years, with the lack of proper winterizing, the pipes freeze, swell, and leak. Usually repairs are attempted by replacing the leaking pipe sections with new copper, but the owner finds there are no fittings available that fit the existing pipe. They usually think that the old trailer used some strange in-between copper pipe size, and the fittings are no longer made. In fact, what has happened is the pipe has swollen to a larger size, and will no longer work with available fittings. So they substitute a piece of rubber hose and clamps, which works for a while, but often fails. You should count on replacing all plumbing with PEX, as it's easier to work with than copper, and will withstand freezing a little better.

Propane lines typically *look* ok and are run below the trailer outside of the bellypan. They should never be run inside the bellypan, because if they develop a leak, LP gas could build up inside your bellypan just looking for a spark, KaBoom! Besides, how can you check the lines for leaks during your yearly maintenance if they weren't accessible? As I said, they usually *look* ok, but you should replace them. When I removed all of my original copper LP lines, I coiled them up and put them on the ground. A couple of days later, I found disgusting black goo had leaked out of the pipes. This goo had built up over the years from tank residue, and would have surely contaminated my new regulator and appliances. You've gone this far in your restoration don't skimp here!

There are a couple of things to be aware of regarding propane tanks. You'll need to make sure that your tanks are certified and have Overfill Prevention Device, or OPD valves on them, which are pretty much required these days. You can tell if your valves are OPD because the handle will be a triangle, and the valve body will say OPD on it. OPD is a safety feature that helps keep the tank from being overfilled during refueling, and it has a shut off feature if a connected hose is ruptured. If the tanks are new, they should have OPD valves on them, and the certification is good for 12 years from when they were manufactured. If you are dealing with used tanks that don't have OPD valves, but are aluminum, it maybe worth the investment to have them retrofitted by a gas supplier. I've heard that OPD valves for aluminum tanks are different then steel tanks, so check when having the work done. While having your tanks updated, your gas supplier can also certify the tanks by stamping a date on it, which lasts about five years. Out of 10 years of trailering, I've only had one person check the date before filling my tanks. If you have steel tanks, they are not worth paying to have updated or inspected. It's time to buy nice new aluminum tanks. Besides, you want those cool aluminum tanks since they can be polished!

Usually the appliances will be nonfunctional. Always have professional check, inspect, *and* repair, any gas operated appliances. It's simply not worth saving a buck trying to repair them yourself, it's all about safety. If you're planning on a modernization, then realize that you'll be replacing all the appliances with new ones. Some may require making cabinet changes, or altering the trailer body for different sized holes matching the new equipment.

Documenting Your Work

The difference between a restored trailer and a Polished Turd is documentation. With proper documentation you can prove that your frame repairs were made, the subfloor is new, and that there's a new axle. In other words, all the hidden structural work has been done, and not simply covered up like in a Polished Turd trailer. If you're having a trailer professionally restored, a reputable company will provide this documentation. If they refuse, I suggest that you take your trailer elsewhere.

Most likely, since you're reading this book, you're going to be doing the work yourself. My advice to you is to photograph everything with a digital camera, even if you think the photos are boring. Take a picture of the rotted subfloor, then another after it's replaced. Keeping a scrapbook is a great idea. I actually enjoy looking back at the photos from time to time, and I'm sure that you will to. Even more important than enjoying the photos, is that you're keeping a record of all the repairs that were made.

Another benefit of taking a lot of photos is to help you remember how to put the trailer back together, or even repair something years later. Several years after my trailer was restored, I wanted to move the license plate lamp, and I didn't know how it was wired. Luckily, I had snapped a photo of the interior wall while the skin was removed during the restoration. This simple snap shot helped me see how the light was wired, and made the repairs a snap.

In addition to photos, keep the receipts of everything you buy for the restoration, and any service you have done. If you pay a welder to fix frame damage, keep a record of it. Save the receipts for any appliances, like a new refrigerator or water heater. All of this will give comfort to a buyer in the unlikely event that you sell your restored trailer. Yeah, like that's going to happen! Keep the receipts around anyway. They're also good to have for insurance purposes.

Why keep all that documentation to yourself? We live in a connected world. It's time to share your work for all to see. I'm talking about setting up a blog. A blog is an online diary so that others can enjoy your efforts.

I kept a blog of the Ambassador's restoration. It was fun and it kept me motivated to keep working, so that I would have something new to post on it each day. The Ambassador blog is located at blog.theVAP.com. I still reference it even years later to remind me how I did a repair when someone asks me. I continue to update it with our trip reports and any maintenance that I do.

Keeping a blog helps with your documentation and keeps you focused. Reading other restoration blogs may help to motivate and give you ideas that you might use in your own restoration. Setting up your own blog is as easy as registering for a free account with wordpress.org or blogspot.com. Either site will get you started on documenting your work on the Internet for all to see. You'll have lots of interested followers in no time! I highly recommend keeping a blog. You just might help inspire the next would-be restorer.

Getting Started

I know you want a shiny trailer. It's nice to start thinking about polishing, and it's fun to pick out new curtains and new upholstery. Here's the deal, you have to take care of the boring structural stuff *first*. The structure of the trailer includes the running gear, frame, subfloor, and shell. It's time to do the dirty work of tearing out the old, so you can rebuild with the new. Once you have a solid foundation, then you can really enjoy the rebuild.

The Ambassador needed a lot of repairs. Here is a list of the major ones:

•Holes in the rear frame rail.
•Rear floor rot was evident.
•None of the appliances worked.
•Broken entry step.
•Electrical systems were bad.
•Tires were rotted.
•Plumbing system full of leaks.

In *Episode 22: The Ambassador*, we discussed how I got started on this onerous task. To keep the project from becoming overwhelming, I decided to break it out into smaller jobs. I never really spent much time dwelling on the project as a whole, that would be too daunting. Instead, I picked out smaller projects that needed attention, and set smaller goals that I knew I could successfully complete. This kept me motivated as the accomplishments added up over time and kept the project moving forward.

The first step was pretty easy. I removed all of the junk. I pulled out all of the nonsense the previous owner added like the 2x4 wood-framed dinette, the old refrigerator, and the household water heater. I cleaned out junk and debris that had gathered up over the last 46 years. You'd be surprised at how much room you have to work in once you simply clean out the junk.

The previous owner had installed wood flooring planks with glue. It was a very poor job, and it may have been done to hide subfloor rot. So it had to come out. Let me tell you, that was not an easy task. I was at it with a hammer and pry bar for days! Always keeping it clean as I went by sweeping it out each day. I was going to spend a lot of time inside, so I might as well make the best of it.

As I progressed on cleaning out the trailer, I started to check the subfloor to see how much damage there was. I really wasn't up for a shell off restoration. If the subfloor were really bad all over, I would have done a shell on subfloor replacement. That's when you replace the subfloor a section at a time, lifting the shell as you go. I went to town with my ice pick, and really hammered it all over the floor, especially near the edges of the walls. Everything was looking great, except the rear of the trailer. I suspected that there would be problems there, because of the severe frame rot I saw when I picked up the trailer.

Time to start forming a game plan here. I'll start by addressing the frame issues.

Frame Issues

Frame rot on the rear frame rail.

The rear curbside of the trailer had a frame rail with rust holes all the way through, with big chunks of metal missing! I'm not a welder and was not interested in learning on my trailer, so I set out to find someone who could do some metal work for me. I found a local welding shop that was run by an older guy who wore coveralls, and had a cigarette between his fingers all day. I bet his nickname was "Smoky", and it wouldn't be because of the metal cutting torch he used! The nice thing about this guy was that he was a one-man shop and nothing fazed him, anything that I asked for was not a big deal. I liked that.

The majority of my frame damage was in the rear of my trailer. Since the Ambassador is a rear bath model I had to remove the vanity, bathtub, and toilet, which needed to be thrown out anyway. I also needed to remove the original fiberglass black tank, which I saved to reuse, but it ended up not working out. Everything is held in with screws, it's just a matter of looking it over real good to see how it went together.

The nice thing about Airstreams is that the shell is built first, then everything for the interior is carried in through the door. This means that everything can go *out* through the door. I know that it sounds obvious, but this is not the case with SOB trailers. They start with the frame and floor, install the interior, and then fold the walls up around it. Advantage Airstream!

In order to give the welder access to repair my frame, I needed to remove the damaged subfloor in the rear of the trailer. When you remove the subfloor, you have to remove it all the way out to the edge of the trailer, where it goes under the shell. To do that I needed to remove the lower interior wall panels. The rivets were no match for my cordless drill and 1/8" drill bit. Here's a tip if you don't plan on repainting the walls. Scoring the panel seams with a razor knife, before you drill out the rivets, will keep the paint from chipping, and make it match up better when you put the panels back. I have one spot in the bathroom that I wish I'd done that.

It's important to inventory everything. Get a sharpie marker and a supply of zip-lock bags to store items like trim pieces and screws, and mark where they came from. Mark the backside of any panels you remove, noting what part of the trailer it came from. Don't forget to take photos as you go along, so you'll have something to reference during reassembly. Try to keep an eye out for parts that are irreplaceable. You'll know them when you see them. Things that come to mind are curved metal trim pieces, vent covers, and door hardware, should be stored safely. On the Ambassador, I have a plastic tub that's molded to match the curve of the trailer. This tub would be very hard to replace if I broke it on the disassembly. There is also a curved piece of extruded aluminum trim associated with it, which was one of those pieces that I instinctively knew not to mess up. Marked and bagged it.

Rotted subfloor removed and saved for a template.

When I removed the rear three feet of subfloor, I saved all the wood pieces that were salvageable to serve as a template for the replacement piece that I would install after the frame repairs. I took a second look around to see if there was any other welding work I wanted done. I remembered the entrance step was sagging, and it would open during travel. So I decided to remove the subfloor just inside the door, so the welder would have access to the frame to repair the step.

In *Episode 7: Basecamp*, we talk about frame upgrades to accommodate grey tanks, and I certainly wanted a grey tank on my trailer. Since I was taking the trailer to the welder, I removed some bellypan so I could do a visual inspection of the frame cross members to see how this would all come together. I only cut off the bellypan from the bottom of the trailer and left the curved transition that goes up the sides untouched. This way I could patch in the needed panels from below, and it would not be seen when looking at the trailer. I soon found that the tank would have to be pretty small to place it between the existing cross members. I was, however, delighted to see that the majority of my frame was not rusted at all, and it still has the original black paint in good shape.

The Ambassador has 4" frame rails. I didn't want to have a grey tank hanging below the trailer bellypan, so I needed to design the tank for less than 4 inches. I also wanted the largest tank that I could get, which left me with two options. I could make two smaller tanks and fit them between two cross members, and connect them with a couple of short hoses. This would keep me from having to modify the trailer frame. The second option would be to have the welder move a cross member to accommodate a larger tank. After some discussions with the welder, we opted for moving the cross member. I was lucky that the cross member I was moving wasn't supporting any subfloor seams.

In *Episode 27: Boondocking*, I recalled a story that Colin told me. One day he was leaving a parking lot a little too quickly through a steep driveway when he found himself at a tight angle. This dip in the road caused his A-frame to bend under the stress. This got me to thinking. I didn't want this to happen to me, as Colin and I have basically the same trailer. He has a '59 Ambassador, and I have a '60. So while I had the trailer at the welder's shop, I had him re-enforce the A-frame by welding an angle iron to the bottom of each side of the A-frame. He also added a plate on the inside of the frame. I'm not sure how much it helps, but it makes me feel better.

Completed frame repairs.

My chain-smoking welder kept my trailer for a week or so. By the time I picked it up he had beefed up the A-frame, moved the cross member for the grey tank, and replaced the last couple feet of frame rail. He did a great job, but questioned me why would I put any money into a beat up old trailer. I tried to explain how it's not old and beat up, it's just pre-cared-for vintage. He didn't get it. Yet.

Subfloor

Required restoration photo. Standing on the ground while inside your trailer.

After getting the trailer back home from the welder, I decided to use some rust inhibiting paint on the frame. A small amount of research led me to a product called POR-15, which is a high quality rust inhibitor that car restorer's use. The product is pricey, but a little goes a long way. POR-15 is susceptible to UV rays that will cause it to breakdown over time, so you must cover it with a topcoat. I used POR-15 on all the metal work that I had access to before I replaced the subfloor. Here it is four years later, and everything that I painted with POR-15 has shown no sign of rust returning. I highly recommend it.

Bumper painted with POR-15 and a top coat.

It's finally time to replace the subfloor, so I needed to gather the rear pieces that I had removed to use as a template for my new sheet of 19/32" plywood. The original subfloor was 5/8", but my local home center only stocked 19/32", which worked just fine. I cut the replacement floor in one piece, and painted the edges with a wood preservative, since it's the part that would get wet if there were a leak. This extra bit of protection can only help. When I removed the floor, before taking the trailer to the welder, I made sure to cut it at a place where there was a crossmember under the newly created seam. This is important when you re-install the plywood, so the joint has something supporting it.

Adding wood preservative on the edges.

When installing the new subfloor, the edge of the wood has to go under the c-channel and the shell, just the way it was originally. I tried several times to get my new section of subfloor installed in once piece. Every angle that I attempted would only let me get it in about two-thirds of the way before it would get stuck, so I decided to cut it into three pieces. I was able to slide the outer edge pieces into place, while the final center one required some negotiations with a hammer. After a little work, all the sections were in position, and ready to be bolted and screwed to the frame. To make the splice solid I used a piece of plywood under the floor, and secured it with wood glue and screws.

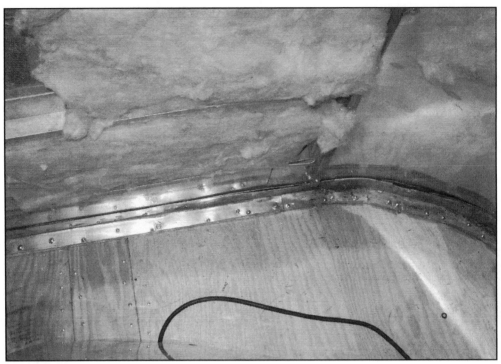

Attaching the subfloor to the c-channel.

Airstream originally attached the plywood to the frame with special hardware called elevator bolts that have a flat washer like head. When installed, the bolt should extend down through the subfloor and the cross-member, which are then secured with a lock washer and nut. You use a special drill bit called a Forstner bit that shaves the top of the plywood just deep enough to allow the elevator bolt head to sit flush with the top of the floor. This way the bolt will not interfere with any type of floor covering you select. In addition to bolts, screws are used from the top of the plywood through the c-channel and into the frame. My c-channel was in pretty decent shape, however, sometimes the c-channel cracks and allows the shell to break free from the subfloor. Since I had mine apart, I cut an extra piece of aluminum and laid it inside the c-channel to act like a large washer, which gave it some additional strength. I secured the c-channel and plywood subfloor to the frame with many bolts and screws, as this is a critical structural component. Make sure your c-channel is in good shape, and replace as necessary. Always use bolts not just screws. I used both!

I did the same kind of work at the entrance where I removed the subfloor for the step repairs. That one was pretty straightforward since it was just a small square and no crazy curves to deal with. One gotcha is to make sure that you attach a piece of aluminum to the bottom of the plywood at the step area to protect it from the elements. If you look underneath the step area, the part that the step folds into is the back of the plywood floor, so don't forget to aluminize it!

Finally, all the structural work was done. I had a strong frame, a good subfloor, and I was ready to start rebuilding. Normally, I would suggest doing the axels now, or at the same time as the welding. I did not have my axles ready to go at this point. It will come later don't worry!

Entrance step outrigger repaired, ready for new subflooring.

Flooring

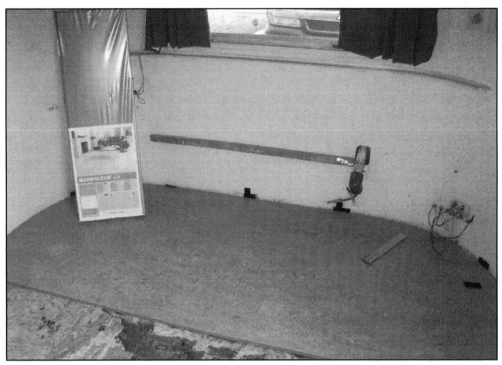

Marmoleum Click flooring.

There are many types of flooring systems to choose from including carpet, stick tiles, sheet flooring, or a click-together flooring system. Carpet was never considered, because we didn't want to track in dirt while camping, and have to deal with a vacuum cleaner. I had some experience in my previous trailer using self-adhesive tiles, and they had a couple of problems. For starters, they would expand and contract and leave gaps for dirt in between the tiles. It looked bad after a while. Eventually, the tiles came loose as they were subject to severe temperature extremes inside the trailer. Sheet flooring, either a quality vinyl or what the Pros recommend, marmoleum, is a great choice because there are no seams, and it's a sturdy material. Technically, there may be a seam, but the installer chemically welds it making it virtually one piece. I decided to go with marmoleum, which would mean hiring a flooring professional to install it.

While I was investigating marmoleum, I happened to find out about a new type of flooring system being manufactured by Forbo Flooring called Marmoleum Click. It's similar to other plank type flooring systems in that it's a laminated sheet attached to a carrier piece, which connects to surrounding planks with a tongue-in-groove system. I installed a similar type of floor system in the Safari, so I was confident that I could do it myself.

Marmoleum Click is available in many colors, which go all the way through the top layer. This means that if it's dented or scratched, you'll still see the floor color visible. According to the Forbo website, the total thickness of the flooring is 9.8mm, including the 2mm marmoleum layer on top. After four years, this stuff has worked great, in fact, my wife wants it in the house now!

The marmoleum needs to be acclimated to the environment prior to installation, which simply means that you leave the boxes of flooring in the trailer for a few days before you install it. I wanted the new flooring to extend to the walls as much as possible, so I ended up removing everything in the trailer, leaving only the closets. I began by sweeping and vacuuming out the trailer to get the floor as clean as possible. The flooring planks have a cork base built-in that allowed it to be installed right on top of the subfloor. I started at the front of the trailer and worked my way to the rear, leaving the required 3/8" gap for expansion so the floor won't buckle when it expands in the heat. Plastic spacers are available for maintaining this gap during installation.

Everything in an Airstream is rounded and curved. This caused a few gotcha moments in the restoration work, especially when installing the flooring. I needed an easy way to transfer the curve of the wall to the plank flooring. I decided to use a paint stick that I drilled 1/4" holes of varying distances down its length. Next, I set a new piece of flooring as tight to the wall as possible, and then I placed the edge of the stick against the wall with a pencil in whatever hole lined up with the plank. As I ran the stick against the wall, keeping it perpendicular to the floor, the curve transferred to the plank. Finally, I cut the new piece with a jigsaw along the mark, which yielded a perfect cut matched to the wall curvature. Using these techniques I continued on until the flooring was completely installed. I didn't bother to hide the 3/8" expansion gap along the wall with molding until after all the furniture was back in place, which left very few areas that needed attention.

The floor has really held up very well, and I would use it again in a heartbeat. I do have one place in the bathroom where a small gap has appeared due to flexing of the trailer when driving down the road, but it's not enough of an issue that it bothers me. Wall to wall sheet marmoleum is probably the best flooring choice, as it will hold up to flexing and spills better than click flooring. However, if you want to do the work yourself, the marmoleum click is a great product.

Finished flooring. Tub sitting in the living room.

Weatherproofing

Tarp used in an emergency during a rainstorm.

Four months had passed since my 'Recovery Mission', and winter was fast approaching, bringing the rainy season with it. I didn't want any water finding its way into the trailer, and damaging my new floor. In *Episode 23: Much Ado About Nothing!*, we talk in detail about seam sealing techniques and the products to use.

Since water infiltration starts at the top and works its way down, I did the same, starting with the three vents on the roof. The vent in the front living room is fairly large, about twice the size of the standard 14" openings, which Airstream calls an Astrodome. Like I mentioned, when I picked up the trailer in Ohio, the vent had a garbage can lid held on with a brick covering the opening. As attractive as this may sound, I removed the lid and taped plastic over the opening for the ride home. It's no doubt that the original Astrodome cracked and broke apart sometime in the last 46 years. I was lucky enough to get a hold of a reproduction Astrodome, as these are not longer available. Hopefully, someday they will be available again, because they are nice reproductions made of fiberglass with a few improvements. These reproductions come without gaskets or hardware. It was a small matter to add some generic gasket material and bolt the hinges with stainless hardware to it. The lift cranks and screen were still in tact, which saved me some eBay scrounging. The Astrodome is nice design that can even be left open when there's light rain, and the screen is easily removable for cleaning. Unlike modern vent screens that require at least 46 screws to come off first. Sometimes older is better.

Newly installed Astrodome.

In addition to the Astrodome, the trailer has two 14" vents. One vent in the bathroom, and one in the kitchen. I wanted to take the opportunity to upgrade these vents since they would need to be removed in order to properly seal them. A company called Fantastic Vent makes a great vent for trailers called the Fantastic Fan. These fans really are fantastic because they move a lot *more* air than the original fans, and they have clear blades that you can see through. In addition, they have a built-in thermometer that allow you to set the temperature that turns it on, which is great on those hot days when you leave the trailer unattended. The original vents are riveted on, so I decided to use an old wood chisel to remove them. I put the chisel between the flange of the fan and the roof, and hammered the aluminum rivets, cutting them in two, which freed the fan assembly from the top of the trailer. If you like, you can drill them out, but I prefer the chisel method. The Fantastic Fan came with a foam gasket, but I decided to use Vulkem instead as it is likely to last longer. Vulkem is the sealer that Airstream used when the trailer was built. It's grey to match the aluminum, and stays flexible which is important for a mobile trailer. You'll be using it on seams, patches, and vents, so might as well get used to working with it. Once you use it for the first time, you'll understand what I'm talking about. Vulkem has a way of getting everywhere like your pants, shoes, and forehead. You know, pretty much everywhere. I believe TremPro 635 Polyurethane has replaced Vulkem, which is getting harder to find. TremPro has very similar characteristics to Vulkem, and is a suitable replacement for sealing an Airstream. After the old vent was removed and the surrounding area cleaned, I put a 1/4" bead of Vulkem around the opening. I completed the installation of the vent by drilling 1/8" holes for the mounting flange. I recommend replacing the oval head screws that were provided with pan head screws and washers, which will help prevent cracks in the flange down the road that can cause leaks. The leaks from the cracks are hard to find, trust me.

Two areas that required attention before Mother Nature came calling, were the two rather large holes on the side of the trailer. The first hole was from the original water heater and the second was from the furnace. With the new appliances that I was going to install, I wouldn't need either of the two openings. It's not likely that the modern appliances would use the same size holes anyway. To cover them, I'd need some sheet aluminum that I received from a company called Airparts Inc. Airparts carries the proper 2024T3 alclad aluminum used on Airstreams, and you can mail order what you need directly from them. After I received the aluminum, I needed to be able to cut the sheets into panels. In order to make straight cuts on the aluminum, I needed a metal shear that I picked up from Harbor Freight. Harbor carries discount tools that usually only last long as your project, but the price is right. While I was at Harbor I picked up an air rivet gun, which came in handy for all the riveting work I had to do. Both of these tools came in real handy and I highly recommend them.

Original furnace opening.

To install my aluminum panels I needed some Olympic rivets.   I
want to explain what they are, but first we need to talk about the different
rivets used in Airstreams.   Pop rivets are used on the inside of the trailer
and are easily identified by a small dimple in the center of them.   They
are considered blind rivets, because they are only attached from one side
of the material.   You don't have to see the backside of the rivet to install
it.   Solid aircraft, or buck rivets are used on the outside of the trailer.
Buck rivets require two people; one person on the outside of the trailer
and another on the inside with a bucking bar.   Bucked rivets are very
strong, and offer structural integrity that is lacking in other rivets, which
is why they are used on the outside of the trailer holding the panels
together. If you look closely at the rivets on the outside of the Airstream,
you will notice that they have a smooth finish.   You should never use
standard pop rivets on the outside of the trailer as they're not strong
enough and will leak. Olympic rivets are blind rivets, just like pop rivets.
Olympic rivets offer more strength than pop rivets, because they have
three large legs that fold out during installation, much like a drywall
anchor.   They should not be used to replace full panels.   However,

they're a great option for small patches or the incidental-missing rivet here and there. After an Olympic rivet is installed, it can be shaved to a smooth finish, and made to look very similar to buck rivets. The shaver tool is a little pricy, but if you have a lot to do like I did, it's worth it to own one.

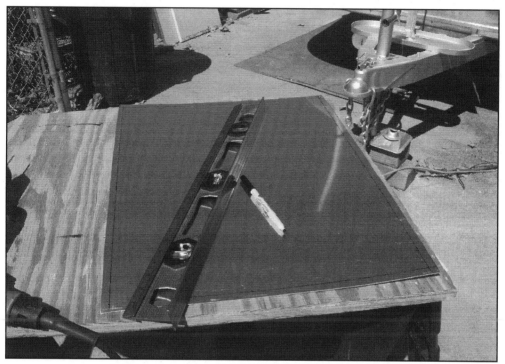

Making a panel to patch the furnace opening on the trailer.

Now that I had my Olympic rivets and shaver tool, I could cover those gaping holes that I mentioned. I used my electric shears to cut the aluminum panels that I needed, and pre-drilled holes all around it with the same spacing as the existing rivet lines on the trailer. I put on a generous bead of Vulkem around the opening, and started with one corner and drilled and riveted around the panel with a 5/32" drill bit. It's a perfect size for the Olympic rivets. It's nice not to have large holes in your trailer.

With the siding all patched up, I needed to give some attention to the door and window gaskets to make sure they were watertight. Luckily, I was able to purchase reproduction gaskets for my trailer from an online parts store. In order to install the new gaskets, the door and window frames needed to be perfectly clean. I used my rotary tool with a small drum sander attachment to clean off the old adhesive and make the frame spotless. The rotary tool does a great job prepping the frames, but it sure makes a mess. I made sure to wear eye protection. I used a 3M adhesive product that I purchased from an automotive paint store to secure the new gaskets. Automotive specialty shops are a good source of supplies for trailer restoration. Replacing all of the gaskets was a lot of work, but think of all the labor costs you'll save by doing it yourself.

At this point I felt pretty good about the trailer being watertight for the upcoming rains. Little did I know I wasn't even close. After the first big rain I checked on the trailer for leaks, and I was disappointed to find water all over the bathroom vanity. At first I suspected the window frame, and removed it for inspection. Everything was dry, so I needed to look higher toward the Fantastic Fan that I had installed in the bathroom. After investigating the fan, which looked ok, I was getting pretty frustrated by the leak. While researching for this book, I read my blog entry for that day. You can tell from my writing I was pretty frustrated. Here's the excerpt from my blog:

2-11-07

Today I was hoping to start on the fridge chimney. Mother Nature had other ideas and has been sending downpours of rain the last three days with today being the worst.

I was meandering around the trailer scoping out the hole in the roof I need to make for the chimney collar when a drop of water hit my face. I was right under my new fantastic vent I installed in the kitchen. I pulled the trim piece off but cannot locate the minor but continuous drip.

Next I walked back to the rear and found the vanity counter top covered in water. I looked up and water was dripping from the top of the window frame. I drilled out the aluminum window trim and water just poured out. So water is leaking in above the window frame somewhere. I can't figure it out yet. The window has a rain gutter that I sealed the top long ago.

I ended up going out after dark in the rain and tied a tarp over the rear third of the trailer hoping that would help until I can figure it out. Later it really started coming down. So I went out with my flashlight and when I opened the door there was about a foot puddle at the entrance. So the front door is still leaking. You may remember I worked on that for days trying to get it to seal.

I looked around and found another small leak on a side window coming in the lower corner. And the last leak is a major one at the front, which looks like it's coming in from the original water hookup. I had pulled this loose and resealed it with Vulkem but I guess it did not take. Or it may be leaking up higher like from the TV antenna rotor that I also already resealed.

All this standing water is not good for my floating floor. So I'm not sure what the state of this will be after all this rain.

This post really underscores the point that restoring a vintage Airstream for a nonprofessional can be a lot of trial and error, not to mention frustration. I suspect the professionals suffer from trial and error as well! One by one I did get all the leaks fixed. The main leak in the rear of the trailer was the most difficult to find. The problem ended up being the rear endcap seams. I used Parbond, which is an aluminum gutter sealant, to seal the seams from the outside of the trailer. The nice thing about Parbond is that it comes in an applicator tube with a small tip. With minimal practice you can run a bead of sealant right into a seam without having to mask it with tape. Parbond has a thin consistency that allows it to wick right into the seam. I ended up using Parbond on all of the seams on the Ambassador, which stopped my panel leaks.

Glass

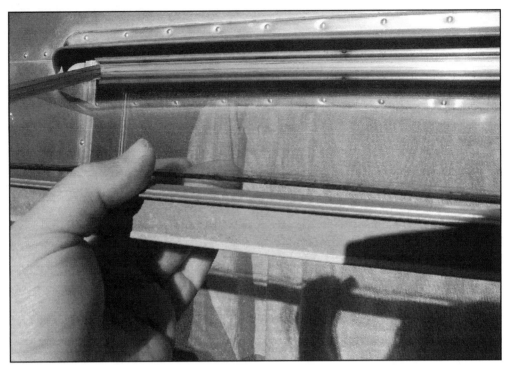

Failed glazing tape allowed water penetration.

In addition to new gaskets on the window frames that I mentioned in the Weatherproofing section, you need to ensure the windows are properly adhering to the frame itself. The Ambassador had pretty good glass everywhere. However, several of the windows needed attention due to leaks.

The first one that needed replacement was the rear window where someone had installed a piece of frosted plexiglass, which was falling out. They must have thought it would be nice to have plexiglass there since it's in the bathroom. Overtime, it had become quite brittle as it came out in several sharp pieces.

The nice thing about the windows in the early '60s Airstreams are that they are just regular 3/32" sheet glass that you can have cut to size at any glass vendor or hardware store. Replacement custom cut sheets cost me around $25.

Replacing a window.

I found the easiest way to remove the window is by breaking it. When I tried to pull the window out to reuse it, the glass ended up cracking. It was better to just tape it up, and gently break it with a hammer and remove the pieces in a controlled manner. Of course, I took the precautions and wore eye protection and gloves.

After removing the old glass and cleaning the frame, it was a straightforward install to replace the window. The tape that holds the glass into the frame is called glazing tape, which I installed on to the window frame itself. In one smooth motion, I tilted the glass into place seating it firmly against the tape all the way around the edges. It was interesting to learn that the only thing holding the glass in place is double stick tape, which also provides the watertight seal. Over the years, the tape gets dried out and looses its adhesion to the glass, which allows water to penetrate the window frame. Many times even though the window was tight in the frame a small area of the tape had dried out, and no longer provided a watertight seal. I've replaced about five of my eight windows, and I'll be doing the rest. The only way to fix it is to replace the entire window.

Newly window installed.

There are two more rubber seals that go on the frame to finish the job. The first one goes on to the inside window frame and is called a bulb seal. The bulb seal helps cushion the moving window frame when the window is closed. There is also a rubber trim that goes over the outside of the glass around the frame. This covers the glass edge and gives a nice finish appearance. It also helps to protect against the elements. I have found that the rubber trim shrinks over time, so they should be cut a little long and pressed into place.

Another good project while I was working on the windows was the replacement all of the window screens. It's amazing how a nice new piece of screen makes the window look much cleaner and refreshed.

Replacing screens is a pretty simple job. The screen is held in with a small rubber spline on the edges of the frame. The hard part is getting the spline back in place after laying out the new screen. For this I needed to buy a new tool. That's another nice thing about restoring a trailer yourself, you get a lot of new tools!

I picked up a spline tool at the local home center. One side of the tool has a wheel that seats the screen into the edge of the frame. The other side of the tool has a grooved wheel that you use to press the spline in place while you keep tension on the screen. Often times you can reuse the original spline as long as it's still pliable. After the screen is in place, you trim the excess with a sharp knife or scissors. Repeat for each window and the screen door.

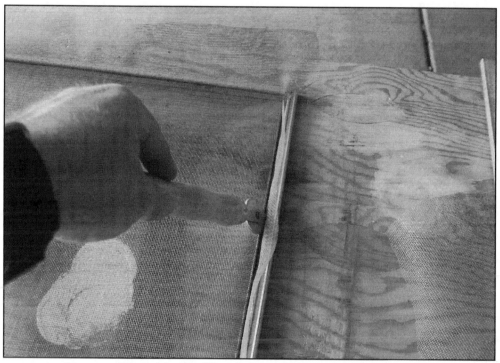

It's not a difficult job. You'll be glad you did it, because they look great.

Wiring

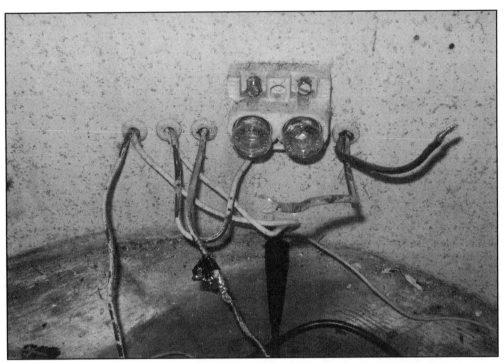

Original 12-VDC power distribution. Yikes!

Wiring a trailer takes a lot of planning. If you don't plan well, it will take a lot of redoing. I ended up doing the latter. I actually had to remove the tub *twice*, because I needed to run more wires behind it. I would not recommend my method.

If you read up on power systems in the Trailer 101 section, you'll remember that there are two types of power systems in a trailer. There is the 12-volt direct current (VDC), which refers to battery power, and the 110-volt alternating current (VAC) that is household or shore power. Both of these systems have specific uses, and require different types of wiring. There are other types of wire to consider when restoring your trailer such as special purpose wire for things like radios and tank sensors.

Since my trailer was in pretty decent shape with the subfloor and shell, I didn't remove all my interior skin, so I didn't have the opportunity to replace all the 110-VAC wiring that is located behind the walls. If you were going deep enough in your restoration, I would highly recommend installing all new wire.

I installed new 110-VAC outlets, and a new breaker box in the rear street side closet. My trailer was not setup to power an air conditioner or a microwave, so installing a new breaker box let me add the circuits I needed for those appliances. This also guaranteed that I could use modern breakers in the electrical panel. Sometimes it's a real chore to find replacement breakers for old circuit panels. It maybe cheaper in the long run to install a new panel. I installed four new circuits that needed to be independent from the rest of the trailer wiring. Since I never removed the interior skin, my wire runs had to be external to the wall, but they were hidden behind furniture and cabinets. I chose to run BX wire, which is armored electrical wiring, since it would not be inside the walls. I installed several new circuits including; a 20-amp for the air conditioner, 15-amp for the convection microwave oven, 20-amp for the electric portion of the water heater, and a 15-amp circuit for the battery converter.

Moving on to the 12-VDC system, I found the wiring was pretty antiquated in the trailer as demonstrated by the 'screw-in' glass fuse distribution panel in the front. That's very old technology! The original battery supplying this fuse panel was a small narrow model that was mounted in a compartment on the outside of the trailer. The battery was long since gone by the time I got the trailer. Even if the battery were present, it would be too small by today's standards. I decided to design a new battery system by installing two full-size Absorbed Glass Mat (AGM) batteries, one in each of the wardrobe closets. I wired both batteries together to increase the capacity. I also put in a new fuse panel that uses modern ATO blade fuses for protection. I needed a way to join the new power system to the original to get the existing lights working, so I connected the two with a number six wire from the battery location to the original distribution panel that powered the trailer lights. The rest of the 12-VDC services came from new wire runs that I installed. I put in a 12-VDC cigarette lighter plug for charging cell phones or other small devices, and installed new power cables for a car stereo and the LP and carbon monoxide detectors.

The original converter, which charges the battery, was missing so I needed to install a new one. I decided on a WFCO 40-amp tri-mode smart charger. Original chargers built into vintage Airstreams are commonly referred to as Univolts. These are very primitive by today's standards. The main problem with Univolt converters is that they output the same charge level all the time, whether the battery needs it or not. Overtime, this can shorten the life of a battery. The WFCO I installed has three modes that are all automatic. There is a deep charge mode that kicks in when the battery charge state is very low. The converter lowers this charge rate after the battery reaches its capacity. Finally, there is a low trickle state charge that takes over once the trailer is not being used, and the battery is fully charged. This trickle charge keeps your battery healthy, and will make it last longer than when used with a standard converter.

SeeLevel tank monitor, Tri-Metric battery monitor, remote inverter switch.

In addition to the new converter, I installed a Tri-Metric battery monitor system. The Tri-Metric monitors the battery status through a digital readout that you can install wherever you want. I decided to hide my monitor panels inside the pantry. I built an oak panel that I stained to match the rest of the woodwork, and mounted it above the top shelf of the pantry.   This is nice because it's easy to get to, but with the door closed you don't see any of the modern electronics.   The Tri-Metric will let you know how much power you have left, whether the battery is charging or not, and how much power you are currently using.   It's a nice addition to the trailer, and it's great for boondockers to monitor their available power.   The meter is installed along with a sensor at the battery, which feeds signals to the panel via sensor wires.   I had to make sure these wires were in the plan.

Even though you can do without them, I wanted to have a tank monitor on my trailer.   Tank monitors will let you know how much capacity you have used in the holding tanks.   For my tank monitor, I decided on a SeeLevel Gauge made by *RVGauge.com*.   These sensors stick to the outside of the black, fresh, and grey water tanks, and use a radar type signal to read how much fluid level is in the tank.   This is superior to the in-tank sensors that corrode over time and malfunction. The SeeLevel Gauge needs two wires from each sensor.   They can also be the same two wires that run to all sensors.   When attaching them to the tanks, you program them for tank they're attached to.   Addressing the sensors this way allows you to use one set of wires for all tanks.

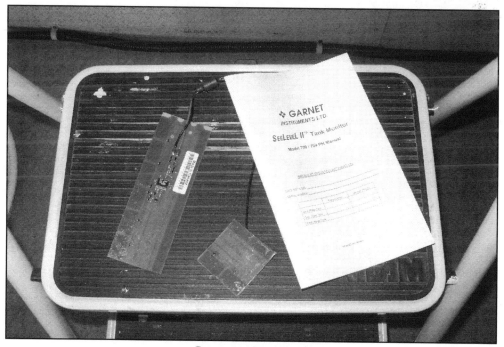

Programable tank sensors.

For the entertainment system I installed a car stereo that has a CD player and an auxiliary audio input. I wanted the auxiliary input so I could use the stereo with an iPod or our flat panel LCD TV. The wires necessary for the stereo included speaker wires that needed to be run from the pantry to the front of the trailer. Because of the layout on my Ambassador, I had to run the wires from where the entry door is located back to the rear of the trailer, behind the bathroom vanity and tub, then back up the street side of the trailer to make it to the front. I mention this because when you have everything out, keep these wire runs in mind. While I was at it, I ran an extra set of speaker wires to each wardrobe closet. I've never used them, but they are there. My trailer also happened to have a shortwave radio antenna on the front street side of the trailer. I wasn't planning on using it for a shortwave, but I figured that I could repurpose it for my FM radio. I had to run a piece of RG58 coax cable from the antenna back to the stereo, which works very well pulling in radio stations.

With my wiring scheme, I ended up with two main electrical distribution points; one on each side of the trailer. When running wires I always would run an extra set or two to the main locations. Especially from one side the trailer to the other. I used some smaller multi-conductor cables to control relays that power the water heater and water pump. These wires came in handy later when I had new ideas on how to control things. Having extra wiring in place for the future is a great comfort. Just coil them up and leave them tucked away. You won't regret it.

I wanted to include an inverter in my restoration. An inverter will take 12-VDC and turn it into 110-VAC. Depending on the size of inverter you install, you can power all sorts of different household devices. I mainly wanted mine for my LCD TV's and the DVD player. My inverter will provide 800 watts of power. You can check your appliance to see how many watts it needs to see if you can power it or not. Inverters draw a lot of current from the 12-VDC batteries, and need some very large wires to connect them. The further away that they are installed from the battery, the larger the wires need to be. Follow the manufacturers guidelines.

I mounted my inverter under the curbside bed and ran #4 wire to it from the battery in the rear closet. I installed a 100-amp resettable circuit breaker to protect the wiring. You should always install breakers and fuses as close as you can to the battery's positive terminal to protect the wire against a short circuit after it leaves the battery box. My inverter has a remote turn on option, which allows me to turn it on from my control panel. Without the remote switch, I would need to reach under the bed every time I wanted to turn on the inverter. Normally, when using an inverter, you need to manually move the power plug for the appliance from shore-power to the inverter's power. I wanted the power selection from the inverter to be automatic. I didn't want to have to move the power plug from the TV and DVD player when switching between shore and inverter power, so I installed an automatic transfer relay to automate this function. I wired the outlets on the curbside of the trailer to my transfer switch. Now the outlets are fed power by either the inverter, or the regular shore/household power as provided by the transfer switch. It works so well that at the end of the trip when the kids are watching TV, I can disconnect the shore power and the inverter can take over and no one ever notices.

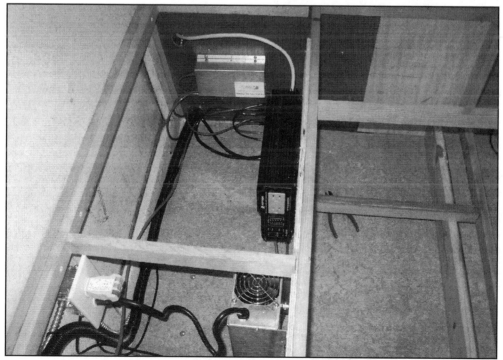

Inverter(black device) with WFCO Converter mounted under bed.

Woodwork

Wood products to restore and enhance.

Wally Byam, the founder of Airstreams, often said, "Ounces makes pounds". Back in the early days a lot of decisions were based on weight. They'd consider how materials would affect the overall weight of the trailer. As the years progressed, pressed wood cabinets and solid-surface countertops made their way into the Airstream line, which among other changes, slowly started increasing the overall weight of the trailer.

On my 1960 Ambassador, the design of the cabinets was intended to keep the weight down, and only provide enough support to do their job. They did it well. The frames are made of 1x2" lumber, and screwed together at the joints. The oak veneer that was attached is only about 3/16" thick. This was the secret to keeping the overall weight of the cabinetry down. The cabinetry is made of oak, stained in a dark walnut, has held up well over the last 52 years.

Over the years, the cabinets started to dry and fade in several spots throughout the trailer. I was able to revitalize much of the wood with a restore-a-wood product applied with fine steel wool. This cleaned it up nicely, and added a bit of color to even out the tones. I followed that up with a good feed-n-wax that really brought out the shine, and kept the wood from looking so dried out.

I decided to make some significant design changes in the kitchen, because the current layout didn't meet our needs. Originally, the trailer had a built-in oven with an integrated stovetop and I knew that we'd never use the oven, since we never had in the Safari. The oven just took up extra space, and we ended up with a microwave on the countertop. Removing the oven would leave a rather large hole in the cabinet, so instead of trying to patch over the hole, I decided to remove all the original wood and re-skin it with a new sheet of 3/16" oak veneer. After removing all of the original oak facing, I laid my new sheet on the frame then glued and finished nailed it on. I used my router with a flush trim bit and cut the holes for the drawers and the doors under the sink. It was the first time I had ever done any work like it, and I'm pleased with the results.

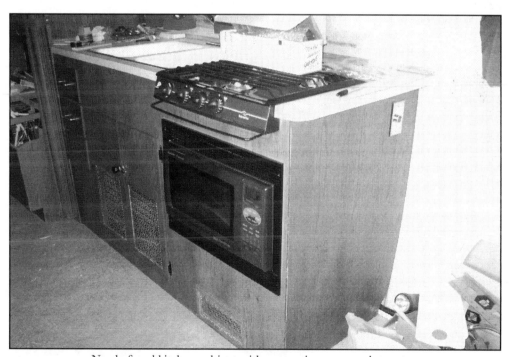

Newly faced kitchen cabinet with convection oven and stovetop.

Another cabinet change was needed because I wanted to install a new refrigerator that was larger than the original one. The original layout had a short refrigerator, about cabinet height, with a countertop on top of it. Since I was putting in a much taller refrigerator I needed to build a bulkhead wall to cover the side of it. Bulkhead walls are curved to match the shape of the trailer's ceiling. Sure, the curvy stuff is groovy and all, but not when you have to make a wall for it.

After much trouble trying to find the right arc, I was researching how to match the shell curvature when a fellow Airstreamer told me about a technique boater's use called the story stick. The concept is that you make a template from paper or luan wood, and cut it to match the rough shape you need. You use a stick and line it up against the curve *and* your template then mark with a pencil where the stick contacts the paper. Keep moving the story stick around the curve, marking your template as you go. After you have the full curvature marked, clamp or tape your template to your final material, and transfer the marks using your story stick. The story stick will give you the right curve you need. Using the story stick technique, I was able to make a bulkhead out of some oak veneer plywood. I'm quite happy with the results.

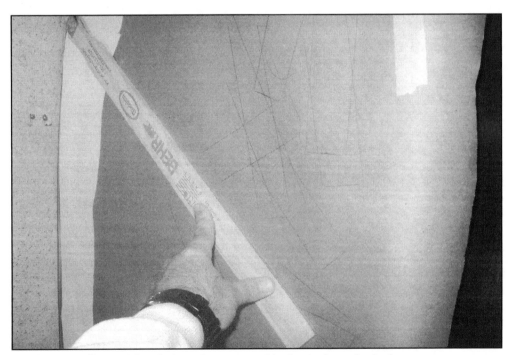

Story stick technique demonstrated in the Ambassador bathroom.

The original countertops were quite worn, and some were peeling. They're made of 3/8" plywood with trim added to the edges to give a thicker, more finished appearance. These techniques were used to keep the weight of the trailer down. I decided to rebuild the countertops since I was putting in a new sink in the bathroom, and a new stovetop in the kitchen. The original bathroom sink was pink to match the pink tub and pink toilet. I wanted a more modern look. Besides, that's way too much pink for anyone! The only small-sized sink that I could find to fit the vanity was a stainless-bar sink, which turned out nicely as it matches the aluminum trim that is throughout the trailer.

We decided to use vinyl laminate for the countertops. Deb and I chose a simple pattern that matched the rest of the decor. After building the plywood countertops based on the originals, I rough cut the laminate for the top. At first I used a jigsaw with a special laminate-cutting blade that keeps the vinyl from cracking. This works, but it was a hassle when the thin laminate jumped all around from the cutting action. I decided to try my electric shears that I used on the aluminum panels, and to my surprise, the shears worked great for cutting the laminate. This allowed me to rough-cut the laminate in a more controlled fashion.

Prepping for laminate installation.

Installing a laminate countertop is not that difficult. It's just a matter of applying contact cement to the plywood and laminate. The only real trick is that you need to keep the two pieces separated with wooden dowels while you line them up. If they touch at all, the contact cement creates a permanent bond. Wooden dowels are great for keeping this separation, but they're kind of expensive. Instead of wooden dowels, I used free paint sticks that are available at home improvement centers. The idea is that you pull out one stick at a time, and allow the laminate to contact the countertop as you use a J-roller to bond the two pieces together. After the laminate is glued down, you finish the edges with a router equipped with a flush-trim bit. It's worth the effort. New counters really add a nice clean look inside.

Completed vanity countertop.

The last bit of woodworking that I needed to do was add sleeping for a fifth person. The layout I was creating is a gaucho up front that slept two, and the two twin beds in the middle of the trailer. I needed to find a way to sleep one more person. After researching Ambassadors, I saw photos of a bunk bed option that was available in 1960. Colin has one of these, and sent me some photos so that I could get an idea on how it would look. I was able to get a couple of Airstreamers to send me some measurements and additional photos. I needed to remove one set of upper cabinets in the middle of the trailer to make room for the bunk bed. I was able to recreate it without too much difficulty. In the end the kids only used it a couple of times, and I wish that I had kept the original cabinets. Now we use it as a shelf for extra blankets and pillows.

Bunk bed built from a 1960 design.

Plumbing

Took a lot of work to get here.

Airstream used copper in the plumbing systems on the trailers they built. Over the years, through neglect, the copper lines may develop leaks. The most common reason for leaks is the pipes freeze and expand when not properly winterized. When this happens the owner might replace the bad section of copper with a rubber hose and clamps. I ran into this problem on my 1971 Safari.

Based on experience with my last trailer, I decided to remove all of the plumbing and start fresh. Replacing all of the plumbing isn't really that difficult, and will save you tons of frustration trying to constantly fight water leaks. I decided to use PEX, which has several advantages over copper. It can survive freezing better than copper as it can expand without being damaged, although, winterizing is still necessary. Another advantage to PEX is that it's very easy to install as there is no soldering or gluing required. You can cut it very easily and quickly with a tubing cutter that operates like scissors making installation a snap.

Generally there are two types of fittings that can be used on PEX; crimp-on and quick-connect. Crimp-on fittings require the use of a special tool that compresses a ring to secure the fitting to the PEX line. The tool is a little pricey, but the fittings are cheaper and smaller. The quick-connect fittings do not require a tool and can be reused, however, they are more expensive and bulky. I decided to use SeaTech quick-connect fittings on the Ambassador project. The SeaTech line includes; valves, right angles, threaded adapters, and three-way valves.

The great thing about SeaTech fittings is that they are very easy to use. The 1/2" PEX line simply pushes into the fitting to form a watertight connection. There is a little mark on the outside of the fitting that shows how far the pipe needs to go in to seat properly, which aids during installation. If you don't fully seat the tubing in the fitting, it will leak. Don't ask me how I know this, but it's easy to remedy by pushing the pipe all the way in until it seats. The beige ring is the release mechanism. If you need to pull the pipe back out, press down on the ring while pulling the pipe. That is all there is to it, and you can reuse both the pipe and fitting if you want to.

PEX tubing itself comes in different colors including; white, blue, and red. A lot of restorers use white or blue PEX for cold water lines and red for hot. This helps to keep things straight during the installation.

The nice thing about PEX is that it bends fairly easily, which is great for a trailer with curved walls. There are 90-degree brackets available that hold the tubing at an angle, which maybe necessary for tight turns. The brackets have mounting holes so you can screw them to the floor or cabinet. It's important to secure the lines every few feet to keep them from rattling when you're running water. I also installed drain valves on both the hot and cold water lines in the front and back of the trailer, which aids in draining the water system for winterizing.

I designed the water system on the fly, and it wasn't too difficult to replicate what was there. I was able to find an aluminum inlet with a built-in check-valve for the city water hose connection. You want to make sure to have a check-valve on the city input so that when you're using the water pump, water doesn't run right out the hose connection.

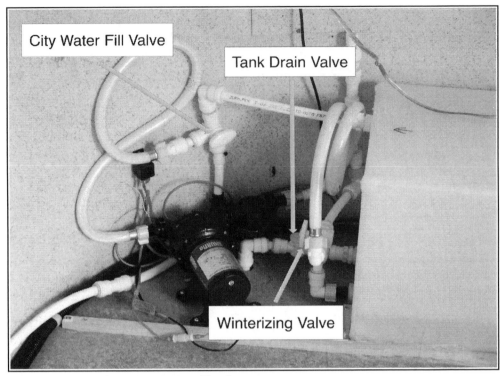

City Water Fill Valve

Tank Drain Valve

Winterizing Valve

Shurflo water pump.

Speaking of water pumps, Shurflo makes an assortment of them for RV use. I decided on the Shurflo Extreme Series Smart Sensor 4.0 water pump. The Smart Series 4.0 offers 50 PSI of water pressure, and uses variable speeds to minimize pump noise. Shurflo recommends that you make the connections to the water pump with flexible hoses, as pump vibration may cause leaks or noises in the plumbing system if connected directly to hard pipes. The flexible hoses and rubber mounts help to isolate the pump from the rest of the trailer.

The picture shows the fresh water tank on the right with various SeaTech fittings. Just above the water pump is a three-way valve plumbed as a city water fill valve. When the trailer is connected to city water, I can turn this valve on to fill the fresh water tank from inside the trailer. This makes it very convenient to fill the tank before departure. It's a nice feature that I was able to add since I was designing it myself.

Original faded pink tub.

As I mentioned before, the bathroom was much too pink. One of the leading culprits was the rather large pink bath tub. The tub is made of plastic, and had faded to a dull and unattractive pink that would not match my modern interior design at all. Painting plastic is no small feat. You cannot just use a standard rattle can of paint to get the job done.

After searching the internet for a solution, I came across a product called Mr. Tubby. Mr. Tubby is a two-part epoxy made for resurfacing bathtubs. Its primary purpose is for restoring bathtubs in homes, but I thought that I would give it a try. The product came as a kit with simple to follow instructions.

To prepare the tub for painting, I had to sand the tub with some fine grit sandpaper to scuff the surface so it will accept the paint. After the sanding was completed, I needed to clean it with a solution that came in the kit. The next step was to mix the epoxy and paint, which came in two cans. The paint was then brushed on with a brush that also came in the kit. After exactly one hour, following the directions, I went over the tub with the paint for the second coat. As the paint dried, it self-leveled on the tub surface and turned to a high gloss. I like the way it turned out, and it has held up well for years.

Cleaning is the only real concern on painted plastic. You cannot use harsh abrasives in the tub. We only use mild liquid cleaners with soft sponges.

It sure makes the bathroom look new, modern, but most of all clean.

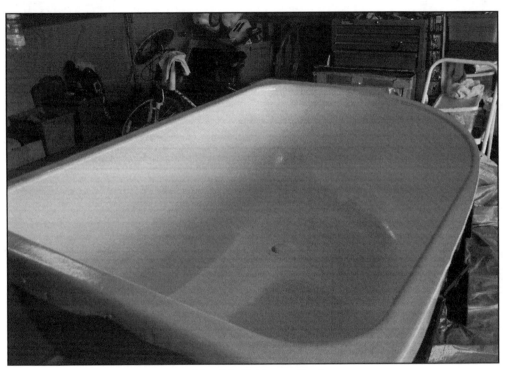

After Mr. Tubby application.

Tanks

Like most 1960 Airstreams, my Ambassador originally came with an aluminum pressurized fresh water tank, and a fiberglass black water tank for the toilet. Grey water from the sinks and tub drained directly on the ground. That's the way it was done back in the day.

In *Episode 91: Tank You Very Much*, we talk about replacing black and grey water tanks. From my experience with theVAP podcast, I knew that a fiberglass tank was superior to a plastic one. Plastic tanks tend to crack with age and are difficult to repair. Fiberglass tanks are more resilient, so I wanted to try to keep it if at all possible.

I had already removed the fiberglass tank when I dismantled the bathroom for the frame repairs. The problem with the black tank is that it didn't use modern pipe fittings on the drain. The black tank sewer hose connection on my Ambassador required a custom 2" metal fitting, which might have been easy to find in 1960, but not now. The current standard for sewer hoses is a 3" bayonet fitting. I decided to remove the original connection, and fiberglass on a plate that would allow me to attach a modern fitting. I had never worked with fiberglass before, so I set out to learn a new trade. I gathered my supplies, and installed the new fitting in a couple of hours. Yes, it's kind of nasty working with a 46-year-old black tank, but I was hoping that it would be worth it. After the instructed drying period, I decided to fill the tank with water, and leak test the new fittings. To my dismay, it leaked like crazy! Ugh! It was then I decided that a plastic tank isn't so bad... Time to design one.

I found a company online who makes custom tanks called All-Rite Custom Manufacturing. They build custom plastic tanks based on a drawing that you fax to them. You specify the number of fittings, sizes, and locations that you require on the tank. Now that I was designing the tank, I had the opportunity to take care of another issue caused by the original toilet system design.

Holding tanks need to be vented to the outside in order to expel any gas build up, as well as aid in draining. My 1960 toilet had a vent output for the black tank that extended out from the base of the toilet. The vent was an integral part of the toilet design. From the toilet base, the vent connection went into the wall via a rubber tube that extended to the roof. I had no faith that this tube was in any shape to reuse, and finding a new toilet with an integrated vent connection would be impossible. I had to find a way to fix this problem.

Originally, the black tank went from the end of the trailer to just shy of the wardrobe closet on the curbside of the Airstream, which resulted in a tank size of about 12 gallons. I decided that by extending the tank *into* the closet, I could gain extra capacity, and have a solution for my venting issue. With this modification, I ended up with about 20 gallons for the black tank. As a result of the design change, a portion of the tank was now inside the closet, which made it a simple matter to run a tank vent to the roof. This allowed me to install a modern RV toilet without having to worry about the vent issue. I got two bonuses by building a new tank; I was able to make it larger, which is great for a family of five, and take care of the vent issue.

Here's an early drawing of the black tank that I had made. The final design was about 10" longer than the diagram shows. The holes are threaded, and allowed me to screw in all the plumbing fittings that I needed.

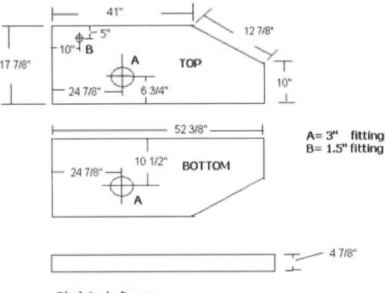

Black tank diagram

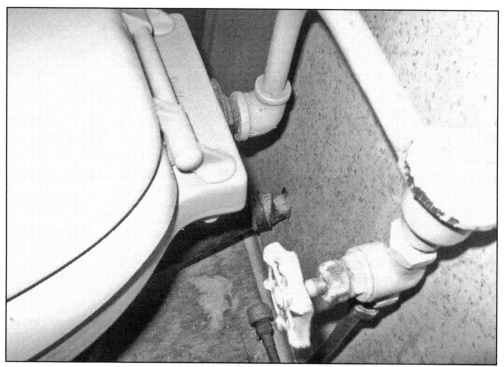

Original toilet with built-in black tank vent output.

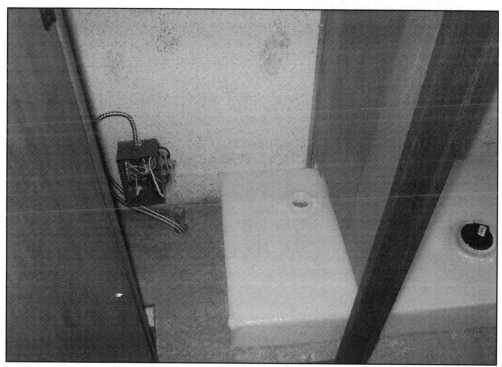

Black tank extended inside of closet to allow venting to roof.

Black tank as delivered. The grey tank is in the background.

The grey water tank was another custom tank by All-Rite. This tank had to fit within the frame cross members that I had moved earlier, while being slightly less than the frame height of 4 inches. I had three 1.5" fittings installed on the grey tank; one fitting on top and two on the side. The fitting on the top of the tank was for the drain from the kitchen sink, which was also plumbed into the vent stack located in the street side closet. One of the side tank fittings was for the bathroom sink and tub drain, with the remaining fitting used for the drain valve assembly. This setup turned out really well, and I ended up with a 25 gallon grey tank capacity.

I did have one problem with the grey tank after it was installed. The tank sensor that I use needs to be installed about 4" away from any metal. The tank was designed to fit snuggly between my frame's cross members, which put the sensor too close to metal and causes interference. So now I have inaccurate tank measurements on my grey tank. Next time I would design a 5" notch in the tank to have a place to mount the sensor.

I was worried how the grey tank would work, since the bathroom grey water enters into the *side* of the tank, *below* the floor. The reason for being side-fed is because the tub is installed on top of the floor, like it was originally. I might have been able to put the tub on a platform similar to the toilet, but that would have caused other issues I'm sure. My worry was naught, the system works great.

Here is a diagram of what I did.

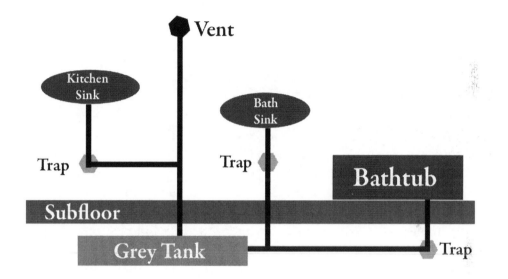

Installing the grey tank was something I worried about for a while. I knew it would be very heavy when full of water; over 200 lbs. I didn't want the tank to fall out when it was full, and I still don't like to tow with it full because of the large amount of weight. During the installation of the plastic tank, I covered the top with a sheet of rubber to prevent chafing. I used rubber couplers on the three pipe connections going to the tank to allow a little bit of movement without breaking any pipes. I mounted the tank with 3/16" metal straps that I covered in rubber tubing to keep abrasions under control. The straps were attached to the cross members with nuts, bolts, and lock washers. I used four straps in all; two right angle iron and two flat bars.

Grey tank shown with metal straps. Also shown are the rubber couplers.

Normally, a 1960 Airstream would have an aluminum-pressurized fresh water tank. Since mine was missing, I needed a new plastic tank that would work with my on-demand pump. I decided to have All-Rite build a custom fresh water tank to sit under the front window in the trailer. Most of the newer trailers, from the '70's to current models, install fresh water tanks below the floor. I like having my fresh water tank inside, and in the front of the trailer because it won't freeze if we ever went traveling in the snow. It also helps to control the much needed 12% tongue weight while towing. Proper tongue weight, along with other factors, helps to minimize trailer sway. This is one of those, 'Check with your RV dealer' moments.

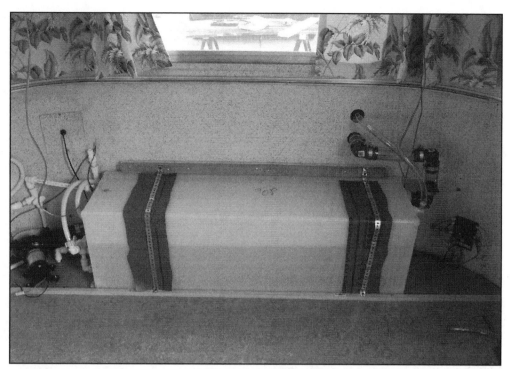

Fresh water tank installation.

For the fresh water tank, I had the usual fittings installed; a water fill tube, a vent, and two water outlets located low on the tank. One outlet supplied water to the water pump, while the second outlet was for a tank drain. As I already mentioned in the plumbing section, I had an extra inlet fitting mounted toward the top of the tank for my internal city water fill valve. It's the kind of extra's you can do when you have custom parts built, and a little forward thinking. All the custom tanks have worked out great. We have yet to have a problem with them.

Axles

Dad helping to measure for the new axles.

1961 marked the transition year for Airstream on axles. Prior to that year, the axles were leaf spring axles, which are still widely used today, but not on Airstreams. During exotic excursions of the Airstream caravans the leaf spring axles suffered a lot of problems, slowing the travels. They were the reason for many breakdowns. There had to be a better way and Airstream found it, the Dura-Torque torsion axle.

The Dura-Torque axles are made with fewer parts than a leaf spring axle. The manufacturer freezes rubber rods and places them inside the axle tube. When the rubber rods thaw, they expand inside the axle tube, and form a rubber suspension. The construction allows for independent wheel suspension, greatly cushioning the trailer as it rolls down the road. Over decades, these rods become hard and wear out, and the axle must be replaced.

The Ambassador is a 1960 Airstream, so it had leaf spring axles. I'm sure they could have been repaired in the restoration, but I wanted to go with rubber-torsion axles. I decided on a pair of torsion axles with a disc brake option manufactured by the Dexter Axle Company. Just like in a car, disc brakes offer superior stopping power for the trailer. Inside the trailer you install an electric/hydraulic pump that takes the signals from the brake controller in the tow vehicle, and turns it into hydraulic pressure to engage the brakes. I recommend this upgrade.

Dexter E/H brake actuator.

To get started, Dexter sent me an order form that I had to complete. There were a lot of questions and measurements that I needed to have answers for. The first thing I did was head over to Dexter's website, dexteraxle.com, to read everything I could about axles. They have a resource library that's really good. It really helps to know the terminology when you are working with them.

I'll go over the specification of my order, and try to explain each component.

#10 Axle w/camber
Hubface: 75.38″
Hydraulic Disc brakes
"A" Spindle

EZ-Lube
6-5.50 hub
32 degree down trail
RC 3000lbs
Low Profile Reverse mounting brackets
OB 58.38″
Side-mount hangers

#10 axle is their specification for the size.   Normally, their #10 axle comes with five-bolt pattern hubs. Airstream uses six bolt hubs, so I specified the Type 'A' spindle that increased the size of the brakes/ spindle, and allowed for the six-bolt hub. The six-bolt hub was important to match my new wheels.

Hubface is the distance between hub-to-hub where the tires bolt.

EZ-Lube referrers to a grease zerk fitting to easily add grease to the bearings.

6 on 5.5″ spacing is the wheel bolt pattern. The bolt spacing is measured from the center of one bolt hole across the diameter, to the center of the other bolt hole.

32 degree down trail is the start angle on the torsion arm. Usually Airstream uses 22.5, but I wanted a little more height.   Here was an opportunity to make a custom change.

RC is the weight rating of the axle. After weighing my trailer; 4100lbs w/ o the AC, couch, or water tank, I decided on a total capacity of 6000lbs.

Low-profile reverse brackets. Dexters standard mounting bracket is exactly opposite of what Airstream used on their torsion installations. By specifying reverse mount, side mount, you can get brackets orientated the way the original ones are. (Not that the holes will line up though.)

OB is the outside bracket, which is the outside frame to outside frame measurement.

Side mount hangers refers to the mounting orientation of the brackets as mentioned above.

Keep in mind, these are *my* measurements and specifications yours *will* be different. You should consult a local dealer to help you with this. It's critical.

I had the axles dropped shipped directly to my welder. Once the axles were delivered, I took my trailer down to his shop where he installed them for me. After seeing the damage my frame had when I purchased it, I was worried how it would handle having these new axles welded on. I discussed this with my welder, and we decided to weld a piece of angle iron along the frame rail where the axles would be installed. This provided extra support and load distribution across more of the frame. After four years of use, they have worked great.

I ended up with about three to four inches of increased ride height. I wanted this extra height because when I was backing into my driveway, it was very close to scraping the dump valve. Now I have plenty of room. The increased ride height was made possible from specific design changes I made along the way, such as increasing the down trail angle, and adding the frame supports. These are just some examples of what you can do when you're doing a custom restoration.

Propane

Sometimes I would call the propane lines pro-pain, because I had so much trouble putting them in. This is another area of expertise I had to learn. Maybe it wasn't exactly because I was having extra trouble, more likely it was because I was getting to the end of a very long restoration, and I wasn't having fun anymore. The work day in and day out was getting tiresome, but I knew if *I didn't finish*, the work would never be done. That can happen, and it's never a good thing, because you can start taking short cuts. Don't fall in that trap. In *Episode 132: Being Frank Malkovich*, we talk about replacing propane lines.

Replacing the propane lines is not really an optional step in my book. Hey, I can actually say that now since *this* is my book. I was installing all new appliances, and I didn't want to have any problems because I didn't replace the original gas lines. Remember the 'goo' I mentioned earlier in the chapter?

I chose to install a 1/2" main copper line down the center of the trailer, and then used 3/8" copper for the branches to the appliances. I have a propane refrigerator, stovetop, and water heater/furnace.

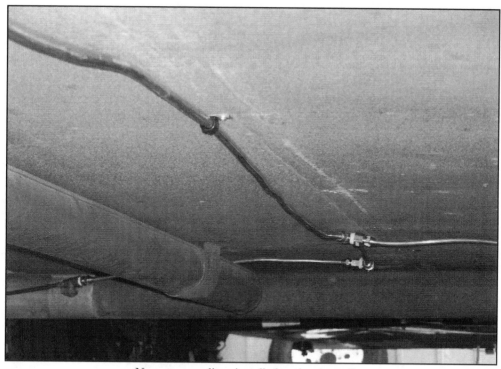

New propane lines installed under the trailer.

There were some special tools I needed to work with copper. I needed a tubing cutter to make the pipe lengths that I needed, and a tubing bender, that looks like a spring that goes over the copper pipe. If you bend the pipe without the tool it kinks, and you don't want to do that. The last tool I needed was a flaring tool, which lets you make the flairs necessary for the appliance connections.

I purchased a new dual auto-switching propane regulator from a local RV store. This is another item you don't want to skimp on. There is no reason to try to keep using a vintage regulator. There are diaphragms in the regulator that keep the pressure to a specific value the appliances need. If the pressure is too high or too low you'll have issues. The new dual regular allowed me to hook up my two new seven-gallon aluminum Worthington propane tanks. You can't have an aluminum trailer without aluminum tanks! The regulator is an auto-switch over type. If one propane tank empties, it sets a red flag on the regulator, and changes service to the second tank automatically.

As I said, on the Ambassador, I ran a main line down the center of the bottom of the trailer. I came off the main line to feed the refrigerator and the stovetop. After the kitchen, the copper line continued down the length of the bellypan to the rear of the trailer where the water heater is located. Rubberized metal clamps and rivets were used to support the copper lines to the bottom of the trailer. I installed gas shut-off valves on the bottom of the trailer at each appliance entry point. This way if I have a problem with one appliance, I can turn the gas off and continue using the others. Never use flexible propane lines that you may see at home improvement stores. These are not designed for the constant vibration they will be subject to in a mobile application.

Holes were made through the bellypan and subfloor to allow the propane lines to enter the trailer right below the appliance. The idea is to keep the lines inside the trailer as short as required to get the job done. I protected the lines with a short piece of rubber tube where it passes through the flooring.

If you decide to flair your own propane lines, don't forget to put the nuts on the line *before* you flair the ends! You'll only make that mistake once! Don't ask me how I know. When attaching the propane line to the appliance, I made sure to always use two wrenches. Use one wrench on the propane line, and the other on the appliance fitting. Copper is soft and has a tendency to twist.

When I was finished installing everything I tested the lines for leaks. The quick test was to turn on the gas at the tank for about 15 seconds or so then turn the valve back off. I watched the gas indicator on the regulator. If it changed to red that would have meant a leak somewhere. I was going to say bad leak, but I think that all propane leaks are bad. It's a good thing they add a scent to the propane gas so we can smell it. It smells like rotten eggs. After I passed that test, I used a leak detection solution from a local RV shop. The leak detection solution comes in a spray bottle that you use on every joint and connection. After spraying, I waited at least 30 seconds to see if bubbles started to appear. In a few cases they started bubbling, and I had to tighten the connections with two wrenches. They really needed to be tight. When they were tight enough, there wasn't any more bubbles.

I try to check for leaks in the propane system once a year. It's not too hard, and helps me sleep better. In addition to the annual leak testing, I installed an LP gas detector in the trailer.

LP gas can be dangerous. Consult a professional when in doubt.

Gas leak detection spray.

Refrigerator

Fitting the refrigerator in the kitchen.

The refrigerator I chose is a Dometic 1062RBS with black stainless steel doors. I wanted this model because it's a good size for our family, and it switches between gas and electric modes automatically. This is very convenient when leaving a campground.

RV refrigerators work by heating ammonia with a gas flame or electric heating element. There is a chemical reaction that cools the refrigerator through evaporation. It is critical to have proper air flow through the rear fins of the refrigerator to cool them during this process. Usually this is done through convection, without the need for external fans. If your refrigerator is installed right, you won't need any cooling fans. Some RV stores sell after market fans that can be installed in the refrigerator chimney, and they come with a small solar panel to power them. This small addition of air movement helps cool the refrigerator down during extreme hot weather. On the Ambassador, I installed two 12-VDC fans in my chimney, and ran the wiring to my control panel in the pantry. I can turn them on whenever I need them. Fortunately, I have never needed them, even when camping in temperatures above 100° F.

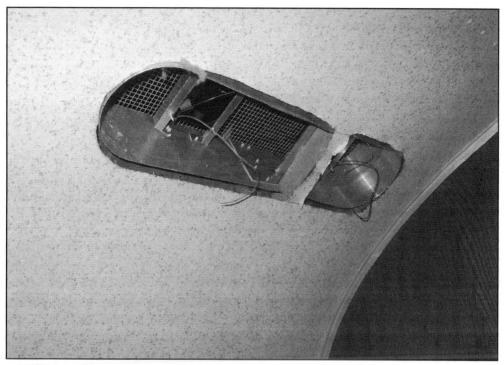

New roof vent fitted with two 12-VDC fans for additional cooling.

The original refrigerator in my Ambassador was a gas only model. It worked by taking in cool air from inside the trailer and it exhausted the combustion fumes via an in-wall tube, which exited at a small chimney on the roof. This configuration was too small for the refrigerator I wanted, because it wouldn't vent enough air. It's not acceptable these days to take air from inside the trailer for the combustion of heat for the refrigerator. I set out to find a way to bring in outside air for combustion, as well as proper roof venting for the refrigerator.

Vent created for fresh air intake for refrigerator combustion.

My 1971 Safari had an air intake in the floor behind the refrigerator, and vented to the roof via a surface mounted chimney. I decided to copy this design for my Ambassador. I ordered a refrigerator chimney from an Airstream dealer. Airstream still custom makes these for their trailers. Although the chimney is a high quality aluminum part, it's not original to 1960. This is one of those times that doing a modernization, instead of a restoration, came in handy. The chimney came ready to install, with a roof penetration sleeve and a cap. I installed these in the same location as the original hole for the old exhaust.

Modern refrigerator vent installed.

I cut an opening in the floor the width of the refrigerator and about five inches wide, which I covered with some 1/4" screening on both the bottom of the trailer and the top of the floor to keep the critters out. When I installed the refrigerator, I pushed it back as close to the wall as I could without touching it. This made certain that the airflow would have to go through the fins on its way out of the chimney. Some restorers add aluminum baffles in their design to ensure this flow takes place. My back up plan, if this proved not be enough airflow, was to have the refrigerator access door punched with horizontal baffles, like some modern trailers use. In the end my design worked just fine.

The refrigerator needed a propane line, 12-VDC, and 110-VAC to complete the installation. One note of caution; while the original gas refrigerator didn't require any power at all to run, the newer ones need 12-VDC for their control boards. If you run your trailer battery dead, the refrigerator may shut down.

Rear of refrigerator against wall, forcing proper airflow.

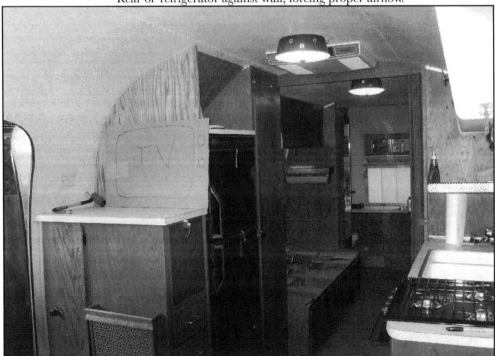

Photo of kitchen after refrigerator and stove top installed. Complete with a cardboard TV template. A *really* flat screen!

Heat Pump

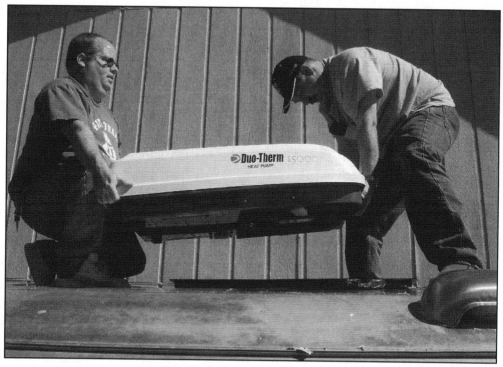

Installing the heat pump over the drain pan.
(Me on the left, my brother, Chuck, on the right.)

A lot of people who restore vintage Airstreams are against installing air conditioners. They say it ruins the silhouette of an iconic trailer. They'll also be hanging out with me in my Airstream on a hot day, because I'll be blasting 15,000 BTU's of crisp cold air! Seriously, like I mentioned before, I like modern comforts, and to me camping in a metal box when its 100°F outside is not comfortable.

For the Ambassador, I decided on a Dometic Penguin 15k BTU Heat Pump model with the Comfort Control Center option. A heat pump is a heater and air conditioner all in one unit. It really makes it nice to keep the chill off at night and early morning using the heat pump. They generally work well down to about 40°F, and will help save propane since you won't have to run your furnace as much.

Most models of RV air conditioners use a dial thermostat on the unit itself. The dial controls the temperature setting by rotating it from warm to cold. I had one of these in my Safari, and it worked ok, but if we were gone for the day sightseeing, we'd come back to a cold trailer. The Comfort Control Center is essentially an external thermostat for the air conditioner and heater, which lets you set the temperature you want just like in your home. It even turns the fan off when it's not needed. I highly recommend this option.

During normal operation, the air conditioner will produce a great deal of condensation. Since an Airstream is curved, the condensation will run down the sides of the trailer and eventually leave streaks. To remedy this problem, the Airstream factory starting building a drain pan for the air conditioner to rest in. The drain pan collects the condensation from the air conditioner, and diverts it to a drain tube inside the trailer that exits the bottom. As far as I know, there is only one drain pan made for Airstreams, and you can get it from an Airstream dealer. It's curved to match the shape of the roof, and it only works with one make of air conditioner; the Penguin made by Dometic.

Air conditioners are installed in a standard 14" x 14" roof opening that has been re-enforced to hold the weight of an air conditioner. I decided to use the middle vent on my Ambassador. I removed the fan that was previously installed, and braced the opening with some 2x4" pieces that I cut and shaped to the curve of the roof. Some people choose to use aluminum instead of wood. Either would be a good choice, but the aluminum would hold up better to water damage. It shouldn't leak anymore anyway, right?

A heat pump requires a lot of wiring for proper operation. During the wiring phase I ran a dedicated 110-VAC 20-amp circuit to the roof vent, along with a 12-VDC power source. The other wires that I needed to run to the vent were a special cable (looks like a phone cord, but it's wired differently) for the Comfort Control Center, and a pair of wires for the furnace. A nice feature of the Comfort Control Center is that it can be programmed to control the trailer's furnace. You'll need the extra set of wires in place for that; they wire to the furnace thermostat connection. Here is a tip I wish I had known about. I was following the instructions step by step during the installation and connected the furnace control wiring. However, the last step, *after* the 100 lb. unit was installed on the roof, was to remove the air conditioner cover, and set a dip-switch for the furnace control. This would have been much easier to do when it was on the ground!

Besides the wiring you'll also need a drain tube at the vent opening. I installed a 5/8" rubber tube for my drain. Since I never had the interior roof sections off, which would be the best time to install these types of things, I had to install the tube with the ceiling in place. I ended up running the drain tube from the top of the pantry to the vent opening. From the pantry, it was a simple matter of taking the drain tube all the way down through the floor. The hardest part was making sure there wasn't any kinks or low spots in tube that would let the water back up and drip inside the trailer. This happened a couple of times until I could reposition it. You'll be surprised just how much condensation drains out.

Now that everything was in place in the vent opening, it was time to prepare the roof. The air conditioner has a rubber gasket on the bottom of it that forms a weatherproof seal on the top of the trailer. Since I'm installing a drain pan I needed to seal that joint as well. I decided to use my trusty tube of Vulkem and make a nice bead around the vent opening. In one smooth motion, I lowered the drain pan in place. The drain pan is nothing more than a formed plastic pan with a drain tube connection on it. The drain pan is now ready, waiting for the air conditioner.

Now for the hard part, getting the 104 lb. air conditioner on the roof. I needed some help! I heard that my brothers were coming to town, so I decide to enlist their help. It was more like a draft. I needed a way for my brothers and me to safely lift the heat pump on the roof, without damaging it or us. In addition, I was trying to figure out how to lean the ladder on the trailer without scratching it, when I noticed one of my kid's swimming pool noodles in the shed. The noodles are made of foam and are about four feet long with a hole in the center. I cut one in half, and slit it down one edge. This was perfect for wrapping around each leg of the ladder. With the foam noodle in place, I could position the ladder on the trailer and not worry about scratching it. To this day, my daughter still gives me a bad time about ruining her pool noodle! I placed two ladders next to each other on the trailer. My brother, Chuck, and I simply walked up the ladders with the heat pump and set it on the edge of the roof. Then we climbed on the roof, picked up the heat pump, and set it on the drain pan. If we needed to make any adjustments, we lifted it up again and set it back down carefully. I realize that I just made this sound really easy, but its very dangerous work. Seek some professional help before attempting it yourself.

Inside the trailer I installed the last few bolts for the mounting bracket. As I tightened the bolts, I looked at the heat pump seal and made sure that it compressed evenly all the way around. The only thing left to do was wire up the 110-VAC, and the control wires for the thermostat. The final step was installing the internal cover. Cool air at last!

Water Heater

Stock white door(left) with optional grey door(right).

The original water heater that I installed was a combination water heater and furnace. The unit is called Twin Temp Jr, manufactured by Precision Temp. The Twin Temp Jr. is a unique product in that it provides unlimited hot water and hydronic heating. Heating is accomplished by blowing air over heat exchangers that have heated antifreeze circulating through them. The Twin Temp Jr. runs on propane as its primary fuel. It also uses a 110-VAC heating element to add a small supplemental heat source.

The size of the Ambassador required three heat exchangers for the furnace application. One exchanger was installed in the kitchen, another in the mid bedroom, and the last one in the rear bathroom. PEX plumbing lines were used to connect the exchangers to the main unit. There is a valve on the Twin Temp Jr. that allows you to bypass the circulation of the heated antifreeze during the summer.

The water heater portion was plumbed, much like any other water heater, with a cold line input and a hot water output. The unit also required a copper propane line and 12-VDC for power.

The Twin Temp Jr. served us pretty well for about four years. We did have three trips that it gave us trouble on. On one trip it was because a sensor failed, and the second time was because the coolant level was too low. The last trip with it, the coolant tank failed completely. Instead of fixing it, we decided to replace it.

We chose a six-gallon Atwood water heater that was a gas/electric combo unit with electronic ignition. It's a nice model with a straightforward installation. After cutting the opening on the side of the trailer with my electric shears, the water heater slid right into place. Since I initially used PEX tubing for the plumbing, it was a simple matter to connect the lines to the new water heater.

I decided to add three extra valves to the water heater plumbing for a bypass. A bypass is used when you winterize your trailer. You set the valves to bypass mode, so when you pump RV antifreeze in your water lines, you don't have to fill up the water heater with it. I live in California so I never winterize, but I may not live here forever. So I thought it was best to add the bypass now.

Atwood water heater installed with optional bypass valves.

The Atwood comes with a nice control panel with two switches to turn on gas heating, electric heating, or both. There's also a pilot out lamp on the panel to let you know if the pilot doesn't light. Since I had the SeeLevel panel that included these functions, I wired mine up to that instead. The installation turned out nicely, and now with the flip of a switch, I have hot water.

If you are going the Atwood route, the water heater normally comes with a white door. That will never do on an Airstream, so you have two options here. The first is to laminate the white door with some alclad aluminum. This will be the hardest option, but it will look the best if done well. The second choice is to purchase the optional grey door from Atwood, which you can order from any dealer. While the grey color doesn't match the trailer all that great, it's certainly better than a white door.

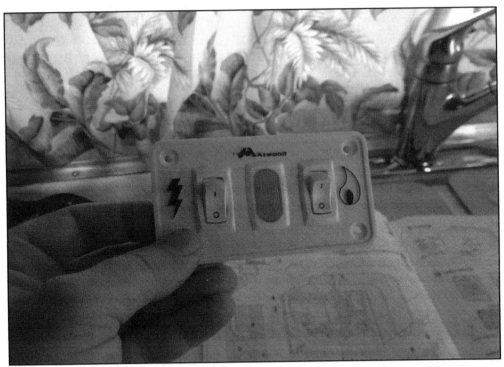

Atwood control panel.

Completed installation with grey door.

Convection Microwave

Convection microwave with option venting installed.

Convection microwaves are a mystery to me. The only reason I decided on a convection type of microwave was because I wasn't going to have an oven. Convection microwaves allow you to brown foods and bake, which a microwave can't do. We only use it as a microwave.

The main goal was to find a relatively low power microwave that could be built into a wall. This one is 400 watts, and had an optional venting kit for in-wall installation. Of course, the manufacturer doesn't think the wall will be traveling down the highway at 60 mph. The venting kit redirects the hot air from the rear of the microwave to the front through the add-on baffles, but you have to find a way to mount it.

Supports added for microwave. 110-VAC outlet installed.

I built some extra shelving support inside the cabinet. This held the microwave up, but did nothing for keeping it from bouncing out. I had to build a custom aluminum bracket, and attach it to a front screw on the microwave. The bracket was screwed to the cabinet frame. I used an additional L bracket on the rear. So far, over thousands of miles, it has held steady.

The convection microwave required a separate 15-amp circuit that I installed it when I did the electrical part of the restoration.

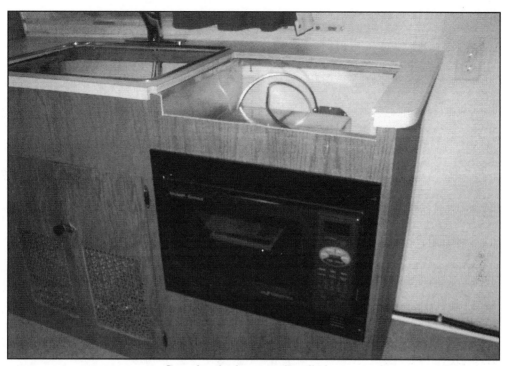

Completed microwave installation.

Stovetop

Slide-in cooktop installed.

We decided pretty early on that we didn't want an oven, which usually have an integrated stovetop. We always used a microwave on our trips when hooked up to electric service. I didn't want to have the extra space taken by a countertop microwave, so I decided to build the microwave into the cabinet during the restoration. All of this is a long-winded way to say that now I needed to install a stovetop.

There are two types of stovetops that I considered; a drop-in and a slide-in. The first one I purchased was a drop-in. As the name implies, it drops into a hole that you cut in the countertop. The advantage is that they are very easy to install. Unfortunately, the drop-in that I selected seemed to be made pretty cheap. It also didn't have an electronic ignition like the rest of my gas appliances. I really didn't want to have to light a match just for this one appliance. I suspect you can find better quality drop-in stovetops with the options you like. I should have done a little more research before my purchase.

I decided to try a slide-in stovetop. The slide-in is a little more difficult to install, because you have to cut into the face of the countertop *and* cabinet. I was trying to avoid this extra work. I found an Atwood slide-in stovetop on eBay, which was nicer than the drop-in that I had returned. The Atwood has an electronic ignition, and a cover that you can purchase as an option. I definitely recommend a stovetop cover because it adds additional counter space, which is already a premium in a trailer.

The electronic ignition uses a piezo igniter, like a barbecue grill, so I didn't need to run any power to it. However, I did need to run a gas line that I coiled up near the top of the cabinet space to give me something to work with when making the final connection to the stovetop. Like the other gas appliances, I ran the line straight down through the floor out of the bottom of the trailer, and tied it to a gas shut-off valve. All things considered, it was not too difficult of a project, and the stovetop matches well with my theme of black appliances.

Chapter Seven

Polishing

Just outside of Roswell, NM. Look at that shine!

Why Polish?

Who doesn't love seeing a polished Airstream? They look great. The shine really draws attention to the trailer, so if you own a polished Airstream, be prepared for a lot of social interaction. People will stop to talk to you about it while at the campground, or even when you're just filling up your tow vehicle with gas. It's all part of the Airstream mystique.

I've always considered the polishing process separate from the restoration work. Polishing isn't really necessary since it doesn't add any tangible benefit. It's more like icing on a cake. A lot of restorers will start polishing their Airstream as soon as they bring it home, which is a mistake. You really need to concentrate your efforts on the fundamentals we talked about in the restoration chapter.

There are a lot of people who like the patina look. Patina is the grey dull appearance that the aluminum takes on over the course of time. It can look nice if the color is even across the panels. At least this is what some people *choose* to believe.

Patina? Yeah right! They're just trying to fool themselves, because *everyone* wants a polished Airstream. So why doesn't every Airstream owner have a nice polished masterpiece? The reason is because there is so much work involved in polishing a trailer. They've convinced themselves that they really like the natural finish their trailer has taken on over the years. You can certainly give it a try yourself, or you can face reality and read on!

We talked in depth about polishing in *Episode 19: The Polishing Show* and *Episode 20: The Shiniest Trailer on the Planet*. Polishing is a multi-step process and takes many hours to complete. It's very labor-intensive, but the results are worth it.

I decided to polish the Ambassador, even before I purchased it. I had good experience polishing my Safari, having put about 150 hours of work into it. I was really happy with the way the Safari looked once I was finished. I learned that you're never really finished polishing an Airstream, it's an ongoing job year after year. Come to think of it, that may be a good reason to keep the patina look! Na, you've gone this far in your restoration, you might as well finish it all the way. Polishing your trailer is like a bow on a finely wrapped gift; a top hat on a well-dressed gentleman. Your Airstream deserves it. Let's go polish!

Polishing Technique Overview

On the show we often argue about the best way to polish a trailer, because there are so many ways to do it. Some people use rouge blocks, polishing pads, or even toolbox polish. They all have one thing in common, they're trying to come up with an easy one-step solution. The *easiest* way isn't always the best way. I'm sure that I could polish a trailer with a chocolate bar, but it wouldn't stay looking polished for very long. Like most things in life, the harder the preparation, the better the results. Besides, I don't want to waste a bunch of chocolate.

When I polished my Safari, I used the techniques outlined on the website perfectpolish.com. The Perfect Polish method is a two-stage process. Each stage has multiple steps. After a learning curve, I had good success with the Perfect Polish techniques. The shine on my Safari seemed to last a long time.

The first step in any polish job is to remove any clearcoat from the trailer. How do you know if you have clearcoat? Take a fingerprint size of polish, and rub it on the trailer with a fair amount of pressure for about 15 seconds. If your finger turns black, you do *not* have clearcoat. If your finger doesn't turn black, then you have clearcoat, and you must remove it before you can polish.

After the clearcoat is removed and the trailer is clean, you can begin the two-stage process. Compounding is the first stage. I actually find it to be the easier of the two, and the most rewarding. You compound the trailer with a drill and a wool-buffing pad. During the compounding step, various grades of polish are used to remove the years of oxidation, then you can begin the finishing process.

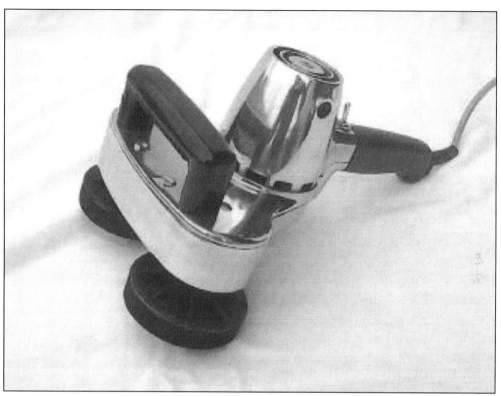

Cyclo Polisher.

The finishing tool used is a cyclo polisher. The cyclo is a random-orbital polisher that does the work to bring out the *deep* mirror shine. You may think that the trailer is shiny after compounding, but just wait until you've finished with the cyclo. A lot of people make the mistake of starting with the cyclo, and skip the compounding stage. While the cyclo alone does bring out a fair amount of shine, it doesn't yield the depth of shine I'm talking about. It also doesn't last as long as when you follow the full process I'm describing. Stick with me on this one, you'll be glad you did.

Polishing Supplies

Drill used as a compounder. Shown with a backing plate and pad.

Compounder and backing plates - The first tool I needed was a compounder. For the purpose of polishing, I used a half-inch drill with a handle attachment as my compounding tool. Perfect Polish makes an adapter that will allow you to attach a compounding pad backing plate to a half-inch drill. The nice thing about using a drill for a compounder over a standard automobile polisher, is that the drill has a lower RPM. It's important to use a low RPM when polishing aluminum to minimize the chance of burning the trailer surface. You can do some damage with a car polisher if you keep it in one spot on the trailer for too long.

Compounding Pads - Next up are the compounding pads themselves. They make short and long nap wool pads. I just used the long nap variety. Perfect Polish sells these, but I was able to find them locally. The important thing is to make sure to have enough of them for each grade of polish, because you can't use the same pad with more than one grade. The compounding pads seem to last quite a while, but you'll need several.   You'll also need a pad cleaner tool that looks a lot like a ribbed pizza cutter. To use the pad cleaner, run the drill in reverse and hold the cleaner against the pad.

Cyclo Polisher - A cyclo is a random-orbital polishing tool used in the second and final stage of polishing that removes the fine scratches left by the compounding stage. I was very happy with the results of the cyclo, but it was the most annoying part of the job for me. I find the cyclo heavy, and somewhat unwieldy to handle. You can buy a cyclo new from a number of online stores. They're pretty robust tools, and they seem to last for quite a while. I decided to buy mine used on eBay, and it's lasted about ten years so far and still going strong.

Fleece wraps - The cyclo tool uses foam pads that attach to the random orbiting heads. Different pads are available for the various steps of polishing. I used foam pads with covers. The foam pad and cover were used to create a base for the fleece wrap, which is nothing more then a 40" by 32" fleece material that you fold around the cyclo heads in a specific manner to create a polishing position. The fleece material will become saturated with aluminum oxide during use. As you step through the polishing process, you keep moving the fleece wrap to a clean polishing position. Each wrap gives you fourteen different positions, which offers a clear advantage over using just a foam head, because once the head gets soiled with oxidation, it ceases to function. The wrap allows you to move to a clean position and keep going. I used less than ten wraps for my twenty-eight foot trailer.

Nuvite Aircraft Polish.

Nuvite Polish - Like sandpaper, polish comes in a number of grades. The grade of polish you'll need is determined by how badly oxidized the aluminum skin is. You typically start with a course polish, and move to a finer one as you go. Perfectpolish.com gives a good detailed explanation of each grade, and what you can expect when using it.

Knowing which polish to use and when to use it is the trick. Polishing an Airstream is more of an art than a science. There are too many variables in the process to give specific steps; the condition of the aluminum, the tools you're using, even the weather plays a role. All of this will become clearer as you gain experience. The kind of experience you only get by doing the work.

Microfiber towels and mineral spirits - Clean up is very important when polishing. The mess from the aluminum oxidation is huge. If you don't wipe down the trailer and clean up, the oxidation dries and is very difficult to remove. I always use microfiber towels and mineral spirits to clean up, since microfiber towels will not scratch the aluminum.

Clearcoat stripper - The last thing you will need is a chemical stripper to remove the clearcoat. If you recall, the clearcoat is a protective coating that the factory applied to the trailer. They did this to keep the aluminum from oxidizing over the years. The Ambassador had the classic peeling clearcoat on the top of the trailer. Over the years, the clearcoat breaks down from exposure to the UV rays from the sun. The only way to polish the trailer is to remove the remaining clearcoat. Chemical strippers are, by nature, solvents that can burn your skin, melt plastic trim, and light fixtures. Care should be taken when using any kind of stripper. Understand and follow all manufacturer's instructions.

Removing the Clearcoat

The first step to polishing is to remove the clearcoat if your trailer has one.   Unfortunately, the Ambassador had a clearcoat on it.   It was thought by Colin and Rob that the original owner of my trailer must have taken it back to the factory to have the clearcoat added, because it wasn't available in 1960.

Pressure washing off the clearcoat.

To remove the clearcoat from the trailer, I had to use a chemical stripper.   I thought that I would try using an environmentally friendly stripper called RemovAll 220.   To get started, I painted it all over the trailer with a brush, and let it set for several minutes.   Then I used a pressure washer to blast it off, taking the clearcoat with it.   There were a few stubborn spots that required a second or third application.   The RemovAll 220 worked pretty well, but not as well as the harsher chemicals that I had used on the Safari.   Those chemicals ended up eating through my rubber gloves!   That's one bonus point for the RemovAll 220!

After stripping the clearcoat, the next step to polishing my Ambassador was to clean it. I washed it from top to bottom with a mild automotive soap, and dried it with microfiber towels. It's very important to make sure there isn't any debris that could end up in the polishing wheels, which would leave scratches everywhere. Pay special attention to the awning rail and windows that can hide dirt that shakes loose during polishing.

During the polishing process, black oxidation powder gets everywhere. It will stain rubber trim and generally make a mess everywhere else. I masked off the window rubber trim, lights, decals, and everything that I wanted to stay clean using blue painters tape. Now the trailer is prepped and ready for polishing.

The first time I polished my Safari, I did it while it was parked next to the house in the backyard. Polish residue and oxidation got all over the ground, and was tracked into the house by me and my dog. This made a big mess on the carpet and floors. So this time, I moved the trailer to the street in front of my house. It was kind of annoying having to polish with all the foot and automobile traffic going by, but it was better than messing up my carpet again!

Compounding

Compounding polishing the Ambassador.

Believe it or not, weather plays an important role in polishing. Polish only seems to function well between 60°F-80°F. At the lower temperatures, the polish just smears, and the higher the temperatures, the polish turns into a powder. The polish simply will not work at either of these extremes.

Compounding is the first polishing stage, and it is by far the most gratifying. You'll see the trailer skin go from dull to shiny right before your eyes. I rather enjoy the compounding process. I play some tunes, or perhaps some old VAP episodes on my iPhone, and get to work.

The compounding process is where the rubber meets the road. It's where most of the real work takes place. Compounding applies a great deal of force to a small area of aluminum. This pressure not only cleans away years of corrosion, but it also *reshapes* the aluminum so that you can bring out a deep polish. I liken it to combing your hair in one direction. Unless you're follicley challenged, you should understand the reference. This reshaping of the aluminum is, what I believe, gives the polished aluminum its long-lasting shine.

Now you'll need some Nuvite polish. The question is which one do you get? Over the years, I've tried many different grades for compounding. Most recently I've been happy with F7. I'd suggest starting with a pound of F7, because you can use it for both compounding and the finishing work. You might as well order up a pound of C and a 1/4-pound of S while you're at it. That should get you started.

Each stage of polishing requires a very specific technique. To prepare the compounder, use the centering tool that came with the buffing pad. It looks like a small cardboard tube that you place on the center of the backing plate. Slide the pad over the tube, and fully seat it on the backing plate then remove the tube. The pad is now centered on the plate, which will help keep the compounder from wobbling during use. When I was learning to compound on the trailer, I picked a side panel that was about shoulder height to practice on. I figured there wasn't much sense in learning while on a ladder, or stooping toward the ground.

I always put the polish in a separate jar and kept the original container sealed, which helps to keep it from drying out. I usually start with a jellybean size of F7 polish, and apply it to the outer surface of the pad. I pick a four by four foot area at a time, and rub the polish on the trailer with the pad while tapping the drill trigger on and off rapidly. This action spreads the polish around without letting it fly through in air all over the place. By now you should be wearing gloves and eye protection. You'll see why soon enough, as polish and wool start flying everywhere!

Next, I would take the compounder at about a forty-five degree angle against the panel, and go from right to left for about four feet. I used a moderate amount of pressure, which you'll learn with trial and error. Then I'd start the second pass, about a half of a pad distance below the first pass and start again. Speed here is critical. Think slowly! You should move the compounder about one foot for every ten seconds. This allows the polish to work its magic. After I covered about a sixteen square foot area, I'd go back to the top and start again. I kept going over the same area until a majority of the black residue was removed from the skin by the buffing pad.

Some panels would only require about two or three passes with F7. While others would require as many as six or seven passes. It really just depends on how badly the aluminum is corroded. Sometimes I'd use a more course polish like G6 or F9, but for the most part, I didn't notice much improvement over F7.

Once I was happy with the results, I'd move to another section and repeat. After I completed a few sections, I'd clean off the left over residue with some mineral spirits and microfiber towels. Rivet heads tend to gather residue around them forming black rings, so pay extra attention to keeping them clean. You really need to get the black residue off before it dries, otherwise you'll have a big mess on your hands. Another important part of cleaning is being careful not to mix grades of polish. Each grade has a specific purpose. If you try and polish with a finer grade, while a more course one is on the trailer, you won't get the results you're after. Continue using F7 until you've completed the trailer. Don't forget the inside of your door-within-a-door!

Technically, the next step is to compound the trailer *again* with Nuvite C. Nuvite F7 removes years of oxidation, but it leaves swirl marks in the skin. These swirls, which are fine scratches, are too deep for the finishing step to remove completely. So you have to give it some help by compounding with the finer C grade. I admit, the longer it took, the more I skipped this step. In the end you're the judge. It all depends on how good it looks to you. I compounded a few panels with C. For the most part though, I went straight to the finishing step.

Cycloing

Cyclo polishing using a Fleece Wrap.

Everyone seems to like the cyclo polisher. They say it brings out a certain depth to the mirror finish. I agree, but I don't enjoy the work. Personally, I find the weight and motion of the cyclo to be difficult and somewhat unwieldy. The cyclo is a random polisher, and you have to move it around the trailer in a random fashion. I found the cyclo heavy, bulky, and hard to maneuver. I just don't like it.

As much as I don't like it, working with the cyclo is a necessary step. Its purpose is to remove the swirl scratches left by the compounding stage. Typically, I would start with F7, then move to to the final pass, which uses Nuvite S.

It's critical in this stage, just as all the previous stages, to keep your work area clean. Any kind of dirt under the cyclo head will result in many scratches on your trailer. It happens quicker than you realize.

I started with a new fleece wrap, and put it on the cyclo with a cable clamp to secure it. I used about the same jellybean size of F7 polish as the compounding step. One dollop of Nuvite on each pad is sufficient. With the cyclo off, I placed the fleece against the panel, and smeared the polish around the area I wanted to work with. I try to cover about the same sixteen square-foot area. Next, I turned on the cyclo, and with a random up, down, left, and right motion, I covered the entire area. You do this motion quickly, which is just the opposite of compounding. As you go, you will see the area turn dark with oxidation. Keep polishing until the all black residue is picked up by the cyclo. There should be very little oxidation left on the skin when you stop. It takes at least five or ten minutes to complete an area, usually longer. It seems to me that the last few passes, as the residue is being cleaned off, provides the most benefit. You'll discover, like I did, that *less* is more when polishing. Use less polish than you think, and apply less pressure then you might want. Let the polish do the work. It's difficult to describe, and something that will come as you gain experience.

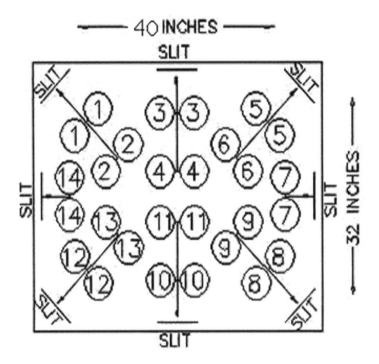

Fleece Wrap polishing positions.

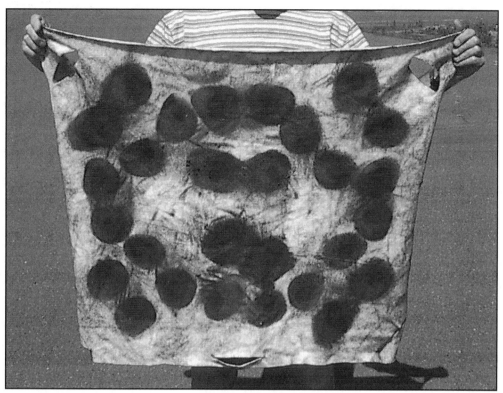

Fleece Wrap after use.

Before you move to the next section of the trailer, move the fleece to a clean polishing position. Don't do like I did and try to use a fleece position twice. The used section is saturated in aluminum oxidization, and will just smear all over your new section. It will not come clean. It just adds extra time to an already time consuming project. After you finish a few sections of trailer, use some mineral spirits and a microfiber towels to clean the residue. You'll need to have all the F7 cleaned off before the next step.

I doubt that you want to hear this, but the next step is to do the trailer all over again with Nuvite S. Some experts will tell you to keep cycloing until the entire amount of S is removed, then do it again with a clean fleece wrap. They want you to skip cleaning the polish off with mineral spirits, as they believe Nuvite S provides some protection for the aluminum. I tired it that way and wasn't very satisfied. Give it a try yourself and see what you think.

I prefer to clean all the polish off with mineral spirits, and then go over the trailer with a clean fleece wrap. Once that is done, I apply a car wax. The wax I use is actually sold as a once a year car polish, called NuFinish. I like it because it goes on easily, and seems to do a fair job. It's important to keep the trailer as clean as possible, especially from bird droppings as they can stain the skin easily. Don't worry when you get a bird attack and can't clean it off in time. It will come clean in next years touch up polish.

I say 'next year' like I actually do that, I don't. There was five years between my first and second polish. I suppose that if I did polish it once a year, it would take less time. The first time it took about seventy-hours to polish the trailer. The refresh polish, five years later, took thirty-three hours.

I know that polishing sounds like a lot of work, that's because it *is* a lot of work. It's not exactly difficult, but it is work. The last time I checked to have a trailer professionally polished, the cost was around $125.00 per foot. So, my 28-foot Ambassador would cost $3,125 to have professionally polished.

Chapter Eight

Maiden Voyage

Maiden trip in the Ambassador near Santa Cruz, CA.

Final Restoration Thoughts

In *Episode 49: The Ambassador's Maiden Voyage*, I gave some final thoughts on the restoration. We also talked about the first trip my family and I took after my 13-month restoration.

How much did this all cost? The purchase price and 'Recovery Mission' was about $7,000. The out of pocket expenses for parts and appliances brought the total to about $33,200.

Lets try and take a guess at the labor. I put at least 15 hours a week for a year. This is a low estimate, but lets go with it. I'll pick a low hourly rate of $65 per hour for a professional restorer. That would make it $50,700 in labor. These are very low labor estimates and actual parts costs. If a professional were going to restore your trailer they would likely have more hours into it, and charge a premium for the parts. At any rate my trailer would have cost some where around $83,900 to have professionally done.

It's not cheap to restore an Airstream, if it's done right. Was it worth it? You bet it was. I was able to use the materials and finishes that I wanted, and I know the repairs are done right. If something happens and work needs to be done on the trailer, I can do it. Would I do it again? I would on one condition. I would like to keep a working trailer during the restoration. It wasn't too much fun not being able to go camping, since we sold the Safari before the Ambassador was ready.

Just remember that there will be challenges as you go along. There were many of them for me. Restoring a trailer means becoming a tradesman in many fields of expertise including; electrical, welding, plumbing, woodworking, and many more. When in doubt, seek professional help, like I did with the welding work.

Be flexible in your decisions. I wanted to use the original fiberglass black tank. That didn't work out, so I bought a custom tank. Think a few steps ahead of what you're doing. Planning is key to every successful restoration.

Take your time throughout your restoration. There is usually a hard way to do something and an easy way. The hard way is almost always the right decision. Spend a little more to buy quality, and take the extra time you need to do it right. When you're lying down to sleep in the trailer at some nice lakeside, you'll think back of all the work you did, and be glad you did it right.

Street side "As-Found"

Street side after restoration

Living room "As-Found"

Living room after restoration

Kitchen "As-Found"

Kitchen after restoration

Twin beds "As Found"

Twin beds after restoration

Bathroom "As Found"

Bathroom after restoration

Hitting the Road

Our maiden voyage was at a nice campground near Santa Cruz, California. This was our first camping trip in over a year, and I have to say, everything in the trailer worked perfectly. Why wouldn't it? Everything was new and I installed it. I know I got lucky. It was a big difference from our maiden voyage in the Safari when we had to microwave bath water. I have to admit though, it didn't matter which trailer we were in, we always had fun together.

We had a great time in Santa Cruz visiting the beach boardwalk, the Monterey Bay Aquarium, and the Winchester Mystery House. The next weekend, we headed to South Lake Tahoe, where the kids enjoyed a tram ride up Squaw Valley. We were also able to visit the most photographed place in the country, Emerald Bay.

Since this maiden voyage we've been to Yellowstone National Park, where my kids became Jr. Park Rangers. They learned about the history of national parks. They got to see bison, bears, and elk. They witnessed bubbling mud pots, and shooting geysers. We've been to Mount Rushmore, the Grand Canyon, Carlsbad Caverns, Roswell, Graceland, the Ronald Reagan and Bill Clinton Presidential Libraries, and many other places. Even more important than places, we've been able to visit family all across the United States from California to Florida. This simply would not be possible for us without our Airstream.

Visiting these great places and family is what an Airstream provides. It's not really about the aluminum at all, but being on the road with family. The aluminum just provides the means to be on the road. Our family has grown closer in our Airstream. Together we discover new places, share smiles, and memories. All thanks to our vintage Airstream.

Carlsbad Caverns National Park, NM

Breaux Bridge, LA

Orlando, FL

Yellowstone National Park, WY

Prehistoric Gardens, OR

Black Hills, SD

Black Bird of Medford, OR

World's Tallest Totem Pole. Mckinleyville, CA

Chapter Nine

Listener's Questions

Introduction

We've been asked many questions on theVAP over the years. A number of them come up again from time to time. I went through the shows, and picked out some questions that I thought would be relevant to someone working on a restoration.

In the following pages I've written down the show title with the question and answer as it was presented in the show when it aired. I have edited them somewhat for readability. You might gain some additional insight listening to the episode. Often simple questions turned into long discussions.

I would like to add that our show is for entertainment purposes. I hope that you enjoy listening to the show as much we enjoy doing it. Any views expressed on the show, or in this book are simply our opinions and personal experiences. With that said, here's the standard disclaimer.

theVAP and the author makes no warranties, expressed or implied, as to the completeness, accuracy, or practicality of such procedure or any information contained in this book. Be sure to always exercise reasonable caution, follow applicable codes and regulations, and consult with a professional if in doubt about any procedures.

Intellipower vs. Univolt

Episode 10: The Q and A Show

Question:

I often see references to the Intellipower as a replacement for the Airstream installed Univolt. Why is the Intellipower used for replacement?

Answer:

The Univolt was Airstream's name for their built-in converter. Over the years the converter Airstream used in their trailers has changed. Certainly the current converters are not the same as the ones used in vintage models.

Since we are dealing with vintage restorations, I'll look at it from that perspective. The original Univolts are very basic by today's standards. They are inefficient, heavy, and have an annoying loud hum when in operation. They are a basic single stage charger that outputs one voltage to the battery whenever it's turned on, which tends to 'cook' the battery decreasing its life.

The Intellipower is a converter manufactured by Progressive Dynamics. Any numbers of companies make modern converters that are far superior to the Univolt. Modern day converters have multiple-stage charging systems. The 'intelligence' of the converter sets the output voltage for the battery depending on what is needed. The system will switch from rapidly charging a depleted battery, to trickle charging a battery that is fully charged. These multistage chargers will extend the life of your battery.

Welding Stainless Steel Tanks

Episode 10: The Q and A Show

Question:

When building a stainless steel tank, what material is used to weld the seams?

Answer:

Stainless steel tanks should be TIG welded with a stainless filler rod. You can also do it with stainless wire going in through a MIG welder. If you use anything less than stainless steel filler, the material can corrode over time and that defeats the purpose of building a stainless steel tank in the first place.

Painting the Endcaps

Episode 10: The Q and A Show

Question:

The plastic endcap inside the trailer is looking yellow. Is it necessary to remove it to paint it?

Answer:

Before I answer this question, there are a few things you need to know regarding painting plastic.

You cannot use the typical spray can from a home improvement store to paint the endcap. When you a paint plastic it's critical to properly prepare the surface. Failure to do so will not allow the paint to bond. The first step is to scuff and clean the plastic surface. Then you need to use a primer specifically formulated for plastic. Plastic primers and paints are available through automotive paint stores. It's the same paint they use for car bumpers that are made of plastic. A nice bonus is that many of the automotive paint suppliers can color match. So if you have a specific color you like it's fairly easy for them to match it.

Should you remove the endcap to paint it? It makes good sense to remove the endcap because it will make the job far easier than trying to mask everything off with painters tape and drop cloths. You will also have access to the inside of the shell in case there are any dents to repair.

Mounting a LP Detector

Episode 10: The Q and A Show

Question:

How do you mount and wire a LP detector?

Answer:

Follow the directions of the manufacturer of your detector.   LP detectors need to be mounted low and away from doors and windows.   I was able to mount one near the refrigerator in my Ambassador.   I had to drill a hole through the cabinet to get access to power.

Sewer Hose Connections

Episode 15: Bringing It Home

Question:

On my 1978 Argosy, the sewer dump connection does not appear to fit any hoses that I can find at the local camping stores. Why is this?

Answer:

Many vintage Airstreams used a Thetford hose fitting on the dump valve. Modern trailers typically use a new standard made by Valterra. These new hoses and fittings are what the camping stores typically stock. You can still find Thetford hoses and fittings, but they are more expensive because they are less common. Valterra makes a Universal Adapter that will connect to your Thetford output and allow their hoses to fit properly.

Tandem Axles Advantages

Episode 16: Airstream Construction

Question:

What are the advantages of tandem axles vs. single axles other than control in the event of a flat tire?

Answer:

For starters, you have more stability in the trailer when being towed because there is more tire surface on the road. You also have improved straight-line stability, no question.

Loosing a tire on a single axle trailer is nothing to gloss over. It's a pretty big affair. If you have a flat with a Dura-Torque tandem axle, you can still limp in to a garage for repair, even if you have to take the wheel off of the trailer. On a single axle, the tire shreds and disintegrates the sheet metal around it.

Seam Sealing

Episode 23: Much Ado About Nothing!

Question:

What products are used to seam seal the roof?

Answer:

There are generally three products used to seal Airstreams; Vulkem, Parbond, and Alcoa gutter seal. For any gaps greater than 1/8" Vulkem is used. Trempro 635 Polyurethane is a suitable replacement for Vulkem that is getting harder to find. Vulkem should be used on the 14" vent flanges, the vent stacks, and the refrigerator vents. Use it on anything extending through the roof.

You can also use Vulkem for the seams as well. There are syringes available to help with the application. Parbond and Alcoa gutter seal are great choices for seams. With minimal practice, you can apply either product to a seam without having to mask it first with tape. I prefer Parbond to Alcoa as I found the Alcoa product to crack over time. Parbond wicks into the seam as it seals it.

Patching Plastic Sinks

Episode 26: The Anniversary Show

Question:

How do you repair cracks in a thermoformed plastic sink?

Answer:

You will need to remove the sink. After the sink is removed, you should make your repair on the backside of the sink. Use adhesives made for plastic for the repair. You can also try using a soldering iron to melt the cracks back together. First remove a scrap piece of the plastic sink from an inconspicuous spot that will not be seen after it's reinstalled. Use this new piece as filler when melting the crack together. Once finished you will need to sand and paint.

Removing Stains From Bath Fixtures

Episode 26: The Anniversary Show

Question:

Other than painting, what is a good way to restore the gloss and remove stains from the original fiberglass sinks?

Answer:

I suspect it's not fiberglass, it's thermoformed plastic. You can try sanding and buffing the plastic. Often times these stains from the UV's etc, go quite deep in the plastic. I'm afraid your out of luck. We always paint them with automotive two-part acrylic urethane paint and plastic primer, which make it look better than new.

Preventing Floor Rot

Episode 27: Boondocking

Question:

Apparently Airstreams are susceptible to subfloor rot. What can we as new or vintage owners do in way of preventative maintenance to prevent future floor rot?

Answer:

Well, more than likely, depending on the age, you probably already have it. Where I generally find rot is all around the perimeter area. It seems more prevalent anywhere near hatches of any sort, the door area, and front and back below the bottom of the endcaps. I think the main thing is to make sure there is sealant around the vents on the roof. They are really prone to leaks as the sealant dries out. The door, hatch, and window seals, all of those should be kept up. Make sure you have good seals everywhere.

Modifying the Grey Tank

Episode 29: Updates and Emails

Question:

Often times the grey tank fills up before the black tank. We can save a trip to the dump if we could use the black tank. Is it possible to modify the grey tank so that I can turn a valve to let the grey tank spill over to the black tank?

Answer:

In vintage Airstreams, the black tank is typically above the floor. If there is a grey tank it has been added below the floor. So as they say, the preverbal poop runs down hill. Grey water won't run up hill to fill the black tank. What you would like is really not feasible on an Airstream.

12v Light Bulbs

Episode 29: Updates and Emails

Question:

All the lighting systems in my trailer have been rewired to 110 VAC. I would like to put them back to 12 VDC. Will I have to replace all of the light fixtures, or is there a 12 VDC light bulb that will fit in the socket?

Answer:

Yes, there is a 12 VDC bulb that screws right in to the same socket type. Check any camping supply store.

Need to Remove Inner Skin

Episode 31: The Call-In Show

Question:

Is it necessary to remove the inner skin?

Answer:

While it's not necessary, it is beneficial. A lot of times we find that mice have entered the walls and nested in the insulation. They have knotted up the insulation, soiled it, and chewed on wiring. Removing the skin and replacing the insulation does a lot for removing the 'vintage' smell out of the trailer. You can gain access to make necessary wire repairs while the skin is out.

Create CCD Look

Episode 31: The Call-In Show

Question:

How do I replace the inside skin to get the CCD look?

Answer:

It may be easier to strip the paint from the original panels. Keep in mind that bare aluminum is susceptible to fingerprints. Even if you are able to remove all the paint, you will need to clearcoat the aluminum to keep it in good condition. Your best bet would be to keep the original Zolatone paint or repaint as necessary, and trim out in aluminum.

Removing Dents

Episode 31: The Call-In Show

Question:

How do I pound out dents in the endcaps?

Answer:

When you remove the interior skin, you can access the back of the endcap to remove the dent. If the metal has been stretched, you'll have to replace the panels. If you are careful, you can get the panel to look about 98% back to normal. New panels are not generally available.

Repairing Subfloor Shell On

Episode 31: The Call-In Show

Question:

How do you replace the subfloor without removing the shell?

Answer:

You can take the complete floor out even though the shell has not been removed. The shell is completely disconnected from the frame, but it's still in place over the frame.

The first step is to level the frame so it stays square. As you take sections out, you replace the space between the end of the outrigger and the c-channel with little blocks of plywood the same thickness as the floor. That allows it to sit up at the right height. When you start putting the new sections back in, you start pulling the blocks out. We typically run a circular saw right down the center of the trailer. It allows the floor to come up and the outside sections to come into the center as we disconnect the fasteners.

Modern Fridge in an Old Trailer

Episode 31: The Call-In Show

Question:

I have a 1960 Tradewind. I would like to put in a modern refrigerator but I have a very small vent on the roof. Can I vent out the side of the trailer?

Answer:

The small 'eyebrow' refrigerator vent on a '60's Airstream is not sufficient for a modern refrigerator. Original refrigerators of the time used the small vent to expel combustion gas, a by-product of the propane burning.

Modern refrigerators require a larger vent in order to expel both the combustion gas and chimney heat that is created during the cooling process. On the Ambassador, I put in a modern chimney and floor vent. The design goal is always to keep any combustion gas out of the trailer. Consult a professional if in doubt.

Updating OPD Valves

Episode 31: The Call-In Show

Question:

I have the original LP tanks.   Can I install new OPD valves to bring them up to code?

Answer:

Sure. If they are aluminum, they are worth doing. If they are steel, they are not worth doing. Take it to your local propane dealer. Make sure they use valves for aluminum tanks.

Can You Pressurize Plastic Tanks?

Episode 31: The Call-In Show

Question:

I have an air compressor for my water tank. I would like to go with a larger water tank. Would a plastic tank work with my air compressor?

Answer:

No. They cannot take the pressure. You have to go with an on-demand pump.

Frame Inspections Needed?

Episode 31: The Call-In Show

Question:

If I'm not seeing any frame rust in the exposed areas, should I remove the bellypan to check the frame?

Answer:

If the A-frame and rear frame rails look ok, you're probably in good shape. It may be worth removing the bellypan to inspect the frame if the bellypan is in poor condition. You will have to use your judgment when you take a look under the trailer.

Black Tank Away From Toilet

Episode 31: The Call-In Show

Question:

We need to move the black tank away from the toilet location. Is there some sort of pump we can use to take the waste from the toilet to the tank?

Answer:

You may or may not realize that the early trailers had the black tanks mounted above the floor. They were built into a plywood box. A low profile toilet sat on top of the box. You could have a custom black tank fabricated and build a plywood box over it. This way you could position the toilet where you want. Just look out for frame rails for the drain.

Type of Aluminum

Episode 38: The Big Update

Question:

What gauge of Aluminum was used in the 70's and what do you use to do repairs now?

Answer:

The material used through the early 80's is 2024T3 alclad aluminum. The alclad coating is .032" thick. We purchase it through aircraft suppliers.

Vintage Vs. New

Episode 38: The Big Update

Question:

Would we be better off buying a correctly restored vintage or buying a new Airstream? Are Airstreams still the best trailers?

Answer:

Certainly we believe that Airstream trailers are the best trailers made today. Just like the vintage trailers were the best made in their day.

A properly restored vintage Airstream gets the best of both worlds. It will have the quality materials of the past with modern day improvements from decades of experience in RV technology. It all depends on your taste, but a properly restored vintage Airstream is a great choice.

How to Tell if Tires are Bad

Episode 40: Bonded By Aluminum

Question:

Is there anyway to tell whether or not tires need to be replaced by looking at them visually? Do you just go ahead and replace them every so many years?

Answer:

The basic rule of thumb is to replace them after five years. You can check the date of manufacture on the side of the tire by reading the Tire Identification Number (TIN). The last four digits of the TIN indicate the date the tire was manufactured.

For example, if 2505 is stamped on the tire that would indicate the 25th week of 2005 when it was manufactured. So regardless of when they were purchased, you really have to check the date of manufacture. You should still check for cracks and bad wear patterns. Replace as needed. Single axle trailer owners need to be extra vigilant about tire maintenance.

Screw Types

Episode 44: You Got Questions

Question:

What kind of screws are you recommending, stainless steel or zinc coating?

Answer:

The screws Airstream used are zinc-coated steel. They are used to hold on marker lights and the end of drip caps. Over time the coating wears off and the screws rust. The rusty screws cause streaks to run down the side of the trailer. It's a pretty common issue.

We put stainless steel screws in everything now. We add a dab of Vulkem that helps with leaks and insulates for dissimilar metals.

TV Antenna Replacement

Episode 44: You Got Questions

Question:

If I'm not going to use the TV antenna, should I remove it?

Answer:

Certainly at the very least you should inspect it for leaks. If you don't intend to use it, removing it and placing a watertight patch in its place is an option. Depending on the vintage of your trailer, the base of the TV antenna could be made out of pot metal that in some cases has caused galvanic metal corrosion. This type of corrosion can cause pitting and leaks in the aluminum.

Just like any penetration in the trailer skin, the seam needs to be kept watertight.

Changing Axle Height

Episode 54: Email Roundup!

Question:

I have a 1955 Sovereign and I would like to raise the height. I'm considering replacing the original axles. What can I expect if I go with a drop or a straight axle?

Answer:

Straight axles make good sense because you have a 4-inch drop now. You would gain 4 inches right off the bat by moving to a straight axle. If you moved the axles to the underside of the leaf springs, it would raise it to around 7 inches. It doesn't look right in my opinion.

Stick with the 4-inch gain. It looks better and won't affect handling as much.

Dent Pulling

Episode 80: Body Works

Question:

What type of dent is repairable? What would necessitate a complete panel replacement?

Answer:

A lot of it comes down to budget. It also depends on how deep you go into the restoration. If you remove all the inside skin, it certainly makes replacing a panel more feasible.

You can certainly try products like the Ding King to pull out minor dents. If you have access to the inside of the panel you can try gently rolling the dent back out. You can expect to get the panel to about 95-98% back to normal.

If there is a rip or the metal is stretched, there is not a lot you can do about that. At that point you have to decide if you want to replace the panel or put some sort of patch over the imperfection.

Best Rivets for Panel Replacement

Episode 80: Body Works

Question:

What is the best type of rivet to repair with?

Answer:

The rivets used for exterior panels are solid aircraft rivets. You will need special tools to install them. The rivets may be purchased through an aircraft supplier.

Fixing a Cast Bent Door

Episode 89: Stepping Through the Oldies

Question:

The entry door my on 1971 Globetrotter does not fit snuggly at the top or bottom. It's mounted in a suicide configuration. It needs to be bent in on the top and bottom. Is there a danger of damaging the cast frame when doing this?

Answer:

You're exactly right. It's a cast doorframe era trailer. I've seen a number of them broken. Typically they break at the area where the striker goes through. You have to be very careful straightening those. You use a 2x4 in the door opening near the striker plate. Then with one person holding the door at the bottom, the other pushes the top. But it's very difficult because it is a cast frame that is easy to break.

Camping in Freezing Temperatures

Episode 89: Stepping Through the Oldies

Question:

How do we keep the plumbing system from freezing while camping?

Answer:

Try to use electric heat as much as possible in addition to your propane furnace. You will go through quite a bit of propane keeping the furnace running. Keep the cabinet doors open as it will allow heat around the plumbing.

For the outside, it makes sense to use heat tape for the water hose. In addition to the heat tape you can use foam insulation to help keep the heat against the hose. Do not use the holding tanks as they may freeze. Keep your valves open. Use the campground facilities when they're available.

Replacing Grey and Black Tanks

Episode 91: Tank You Very Much

Question:

I own a 1964 Ambassador. Where is the best place to purchase a black or grey water tank? What do I need to do to the floor or frame to support the tanks?

Answer:

I used All-Rite Custom Manufacturing. They custom make tanks to your design specifications. You can draw up a tank with the dimensions and fax it to them. They build the tanks from your drawings.

The black tank sits on top of the floor and has a box built around it. The box holds the weight of the toilet, and has some extra support across the toilet flange area. Pay close attention to how it was done originally.

In terms of the grey tank, I put mine in the bellypan cavity. I bolted steel straps to the frame cross members to hold the tank in place. I covered them in rubber so there would not be any chaffing.

Plumbing PEX vs. Copper

Episode 122: It Soaked Up

Question:

What is the proper size for PEX plumbing used in a trailer?

Answer:

1/2" PEX is the proper size. The outer diameter is larger than the copper you may be replacing.

Shock Absorbers and Torsion Axles

Episode 131: Trailer Worthy

Question:

Are shock absorbers required on torsion axles?

Answer:

Airstream is the only manufacturer that puts shocks on torsion suspension systems. If you look at the horizontal shock models, the shock stroke only moves maybe an inch and a half. On the full travel of the axle, the shock stroke is very low. How much affect that has on it? I don't know.

Certainly, a shock has to be better than no shock. Airstream installs them, so if you have the opportunity you might as well.

Appendix A

Trailer 101

Introduction

Trailering is a different world in itself. If you're new to trailering, this section will help you learn some of the terms used in the world of mobile traveling.

The following sections are broken up to help you locate the information you need quickly and efficiently. I'd recommend reading through it at least once if you are not familiar with them. These topics relate to modern trailers, or vintage trailers that have been restored with modern features.

Many of these items were discussed in *Episode 11: Trailer 101*.

Water, Tanks and Usage

Trailers have different plumbing systems than a house. They have to carry their water with them as they travel. Trailers also need to generate their own water pressure when they're not hooked up to city water, and hold any wastewater they create in holding tanks.

Fresh water tanks store the water the trailer uses to supply water to the sinks, shower, and to flush the toilet. Water sitting in a tank will not come out on its own without pressure, so electric water pumps are used to pump water from the tank to the plumbing system as needed. This is generally referred to as an on-demand water system. When a water tap is turned on, the electric pump senses the drop in pressure and turns on automatically, which pumps water from the fresh water tank to your sink, tub, or toilet.

A grey water tank collects water from the drains of the sinks and showers. This water is referred to as grey water, and needs to be dumped in a sewer along with black water. Some places may permit grey water to be dumped on the ground, but that is very rare these days. Be sure to have permission before attempting this. Grey water will have food particles from washing dishes, and if left on the ground it can grow bacteria that may be harmful.

Black tanks are holding tanks that store the wastewater from the toilet. These are merely holding tanks not septic systems, and they should be treated carefully. The only items that should go in a black tank are human waste and toilet paper made for black tanks. The paper needs to break down easily and quickly when it comes into contact with water. You can test how a certain toilet paper will perform by putting a single square in a glass of water. Cover the glass and shake it and see if the paper breaks down. If it does, it's a good candidate for use in the trailer. To help keep your black tank clean and functional, use a good amount of water when flushing solid waste, and only dump the black tank when it's 3/4 or more full. This will allow it to drain rapidly, and carry all the waste with it. Another tip is to drain the black tank first, and the grey tank last. This will help clean the sewer hose before you remove it.

When at a campground you may be hooked up to city water with a hose attached to a faucet. The city water connection provides its own water pressure and bypasses the fresh water tank and the water pump. Make sure that you have a water pressure regulator on your hose at the campground faucet. This will protect your plumbing system from any high water pressure that you might be tapping into.

Full service campground sites will also provide a sewer connection. You can connect a sewer hose from your trailer to the campground sewer during your stay. You can leave your grey tank valve open so you can enjoy full use of the water system, without needing to worry about filling up your grey tank. Be sure to run water to fill up the plumbing traps after you first hook up the sewer system. This will prevent smelly sewer gas from entering your trailer. Toward the end of your stay, close the grey valve and allow the tank to fill, so you can flush your sewer hose as mentioned above.

Even though you are connected to the sewer, you need to keep your black tank valve closed. This will allow it to fill, so when you drain it, there is enough fluid available to carry the solids with it. Once dumped, close the valve again for reuse of the tank. Go back inside the trailer, and flush a couple of bowls of water to keep the seals from drying out. Never have both the grey tank valve, and the black tank valve open at the same time. Depending on the plumping design of your trailer, you could put black water into your sink and tub drains. Yuck!

Power Systems 12V and 110V

There are generally two types of electrical systems in a trailer. There is a 12-volt direct current (VDC) battery powered system and a 110-volt alternating current (VAC) plug-in powered (shore power) system. Both systems are important and have different uses.

The 12-VDC system is the heart of your trailers electrical service. Almost everything in your trailer runs off the battery; the lighting systems, water pump, refrigerator, LP furnaces, etc. When camping without being connected to shore power, your battery provides all your electrical needs. It is important to limit use of 12-VDC devices to keep the battery draw low. If you use too much power, you run the risk of draining your battery so low that your lights and appliances will stop working.

A campground, with electrical hook-ups, provides shore power. Typically there will be 30-amp service for a travel trailer, while larger motor homes can use 50-amp. Both of these services are at 110-VAC. When you are connected to AC power, you should not have to worry about draining your battery, because the converter is charging it. The other advantage of being connected to shore power is the 110-VAC outlets will work. Appliances like air conditioners and microwaves will also work. It's important to note that most air conditioners require at least a 30-amp service. Running it on anything less may damage the compressor.

Converters and Inverters

There are two different devices that often get confused with one another. These devices are converters and inverters. They actually do the opposite of one another.

A *converter* is a device that converts 110-VAC to 12-VDC. Its primary purpose is to charge your trailer's battery. Converters come in all different models and sizes. They are matched to the power needs of the trailer. When connected to shore power, converters not only charge your battery, but also help supply power to all of your 12-VDC devices.

An inverter does just the opposite of a converter. An *inverter* increases the 12-VDC to 110-VAC. On some high end trailers and motor homes, the converter and inverter may be built into the same device. For our purposes, they are usually two different pieces of hardware. If you're not connected to shore power, you might want an inverter to provide 110-VAC. Inverters can only supply a specific amount of power that it has been designed for. In practice, you may find them powering small devices such as a TV, DVD player, or chargers for laptops. It would be a rare case for an inverter to power a microwave oven, air conditioner, or other such power hungry appliance. Inverters are powered from the battery, and will deplete it rather quickly when used on anything that requires a lot of power. It's not common for an Airstream to have an inverter. It is an option worth investigating during your restoration.

For large AC power needs, a better choice would be a generator. Modern generators have quiet modes that can provide an ample amount of power and run relatively quietly. You can purchase generators powerful enough to run your air conditioner or microwave. Air conditioners have a high startup power requirement. Make sure the generator you choose can supply enough power for it to operate properly.

LP Gas Systems

Liquid petroleum (LP) gas is used in many systems in a trailer. The LP gas system consists of the LP tanks, regulator, piping, and the appliances. The common appliances that use LP gas are refrigerators, furnaces, and water heaters.

LP tanks come in a variety of sizes. The common sizes for tanks used on trailers are five and seven gallons. Modern tanks have Overfill Protection Device valves, commonly referred to as OPD valves. OPD valves help ensure that the tank will not be overfilled with liquid petroleum. This is accomplished by means of a float that stops the inflow of the liquid once a certain percentage of the tank has been filled. Only trained individuals, following proper procedures, should fill tanks. The OPD valves also stop the tank from releasing gas in the event of an open valve that is not connected to anything, such as a rupture in a hose. Many vintage trailer LP tanks will not have proper OPD valves. In addition to the OPD requirement, tanks need to be re-certified after 12 years from manufacture. The valves on older tanks can be updated to OPD, and the tanks re-certified by propane dealers. In most instances, only aluminum tanks would be worth upgrading.

LP regulators are devices that connect to the LP tanks via copper piping, or the more modern approach, rubber hoses. The regulator lowers the pressure of the gas for the appliances in the trailer. The common camper regulator is preset to 11-inch WC, which stands for Water Column. Water Column is a unit of measurement used in low-pressure systems, like the LP gas system on a trailer. There are single and dual regulators. Most dual regulators connect two LP tanks, and have an automatic switch-over in the event one tank empties. There will be a red indicator on the regulator to show when a tank needs to be filled.

Brake Controllers

Brake controllers are electronic devices mounted inside the tow vehicle. The controllers are wired to the vehicle brake system, and they send an electrical signal to the trailer through the trailer umbilical cable. This electrical signal energizes the trailer brakes.

The brake controller has a manual activation lever in case the driver needs to apply the trailer brakes without the tow vehicle's brakes. The brake controller device should be mounted on the dash near the driver, so the manual brake control is within reach. It's important to follow the manufactures instructions for installation and operation.

There are two types of trailer brake systems commonly used on Airstreams. They are electric drum and disc brakes. Most vintage Airstreams will have electric drum brakes. Disc brakes may appear on late model trailers, or trailers that have been upgraded. It is important to note that the brake controller must be the proper type to match the trailer brake system.

Boondocking

Boondocking is a term used to distinguish between camping with service hookups, and camping with only the systems you bring with you. Boondockers camp without hookups of any kind and they can camp anywhere they want because they are self-supporting by bringing their own water and power.

Boondocking gives you the ability to camp off the beaten path. If you find a stream and can get your trailer next to it, you can enjoy your time away from noisy campgrounds. The sites for boondockers typically are more remote and peaceful, and are usually cheaper, such as those found in state parks.

If you are willing to boondock, you can find lots of places to stay while on route to your destination. Some truck stops and chain stores allow you to stay overnight in their parking lots for free. Be sure to ask a manager for permission before staying overnight.

Boondocking requires that you conserve your resources, such as water and power. You have limited fresh water, and you must take the wastewater with you when you leave. You also need to be diligent about power use when running lights and appliances, such as the furnace. A generator can be used to replenish your trailer battery, but running a noisy generator is typically frowned upon. Be courteous when using a generator, and respect quiet hours.

Boondocking can be very rewarding, because you can go places that many others will never see. You bring everything you need with you, and take nothing but memories.

Campsite Tips

After camping for 10 years I have picked up a few tips and tricks here and there. I'll list a few of them here to help give you a head start when you hit the road.

For starters, bring some basic tools with you in case you run into some problem on the road with your trailer. These should include:

•Flashlight
•Hammer
•Screwdrivers
•Pliers
•Voltmeter
•Wrench set; standard and metric
•Aluminum and electrical tape
•Spare fuses
•Electrical polarity tester

Common camping items that are important to have include:

•Wheel chocks
•Leveling blocks
•Stabilizer jacks
•RV style 30amp extension cord
•Extra sewer hose 20'
•Picnic table cloth with spring holders
•Spare water hose gaskets
•Water hose regulator

When first looking at a campsite check it visually to see that it is level and clear of debris. Always have someone you trust help you while backing into a site. It helps to have a communication system that both of you understand. It can be as simple as prearranged hand signals, or the use of wireless phones. When backing in, be sure to look up for low hanging obstacles.

Before disconnecting your tow vehicle, check that the trailer is level from side to side. If it is not level, now is the time to pull forward a bit and put the required amount of leveling blocks down to make the trailer level. Be sure to use blocks under both wheels on tandem axles, so that they can properly carry the trailer load. After the trailer is level, put wheel chocks on each tire to keep the trailer from rolling when you disconnect it from the tow vehicle. When disconnecting the tow vehicle from the trailer, the last item to remove from the hitch are the safety chains. This will keep your trailer from rolling away in the event you forget the previous step! After the vehicle is disconnected, adjust the trailer level front to back by using the trailer jack. Setup the stabilizer jacks on the trailer corners just enough to keep the trailer from bouncing when walking around. These are meant only to stabilize the trailer, not carry any load or lift it off the ground.

If your campsite has services, the next item to connect would be your power cable. Before you plug your trailer's power cable into the campsite outlet, you need to check that the campground's electrical voltage and polarity are correct. There are simple plug-in electrical polarity testers available at home improvement centers. Use a voltmeter to make sure the voltage is correct, then plug the polarity tester in and make sure everything is OK, before plugging in your trailer's power cable. Next, turn off the main breaker at the sites electrical box. Plug the power cable into your trailer, then into the sites outlet. After the cord is in place, turn the main breaker back on. It's a good idea to check the AC voltage *inside* of your trailer. There are voltmeters that plug into outlets available at RV stores. You want to make sure the voltage from the park is neither too high, nor too low, while using your appliances. Either situation can be harmful to your trailer. The acceptable range will be shown on your meter, but commonly it should be between 110-VAC and 125-VAC. Running an air conditioner when the voltage is below 108-VAC can eventually damage it.

The next item I like to hook up is water supply hose. I like to turn the campground water faucet on then off again quickly, without the hose attached, to get any bugs or other debris out of the spigot. Be sure to put the water regulator on the supply before your hose. You never know what kind of pressure the water system will have. This will protect both your hose and the trailer water lines. Connect the hose to the regulator, then the trailer. Check for leaks at all of the connections. If it is leaking, try tightening your connections a little more by hand. If that does not work, use one of your spare hose gaskets to repair if needed.

Finally, I connect the sewer hose. You would think by now all the sewer connections at the parks would be in the same place, and easy to get to. After traveling across the country, I've seen a lot of odd setups. This is why I suggest bringing twenty feet of *extra* sewer hose. Hoses come in ten-foot sections, so you can build the lengths you need. I also like to use a clear forty-five degree angle on the trailers dump connection. Using a clear fitting may not sound great, but it lets you visually check that all of the contents have left the hose. Better to see it before you remove the hose, then to have it all over you once you do! After hooking up the trailer side of the hose, connect the opposite side to the campground sewer. A number of campgrounds have threaded pipe connections for the sewer. Sewer kits have multi-sized threaded fitting that may screw into the sewer inlet, and allow your hose to connect to it securely. Sometimes, you will need to push your hose into the sewer opening, and secure it with something heavy like a rock. The interesting thing is that there is usually a rock already there for that purpose, go figure. Now you can open your grey tank valve if you have one. Go inside the trailer, and run the water taps to fill up the plumbing traps in the sinks and tub. This will keep the sewer gas from coming inside the trailer.

Keep a pad and pencil handy. While camping you will come up with new things that you'll need to make camping easier for you. Write down anything you think you might need. Soon you'll have a fully stocked trailer.

Hope to see ya down the road!

Appendix B

Airstream Trailer Weights

(Reprinted with permission from Airstream Inc.)

Year	Name	Length	Dry Wt.	Hitch Wt.	GVWR	Hitch Ball Height
1954	WANDERER	18	2130	270		
1954	FLYING CLOUD	22	2620	275		
1954	PANORAMA FLYING CLOUD	22	2545	320		
1954	ROMANY CRUISER	26	2980	490		
1952-1953	CLIPPER	17	1905	225		
1952-1953	FLYING CLOUD	21	2540	250		
1952-1953	THRIFTY FLYING CLOUD	21	2510	250		
1952-1953	CRUISER	25	3420	280		
1958	FLYING CLOUD	22	2730	265		
1957	BUBBLE	16	1750	180		
1957	WANDERER	18	2190	330		
1957	CARAVANNER	22	2485	260		
1957	CARAVANNER S""	22	2800	270		
1957	FLYING CLOUD	22	2730	300		
1957	OVERLANDER	26	3170	260		
1957	SOVEREIGN OF THE ROAD	30	3860	355		
1955	WANDERER	18	2130	270		
1955	OVERLANDER	26	3297	340		
1961	CARAVEL	18	2250	300		17.5
1961	SAFARI	22 TWIN & DOUBLE	2900	390		19.5
1961	TRADE WIND	24	3130	340		19.5
1961	OVERLANDER	26 TWIN & DOUBLE	3750	380		19.5
1961	AMBASSADOR	28 TWIN & DOUBLE	3900	470		19.5
1961	SOVEREIGN	30	4050	470		19.5
1962	BAMBI	16	1875	200		17.5
1962	GLOBE TROTTER	19	2770	400		19.5
1962	SAFARI	22 TWIN & DOUBLE	3050	420		19.5
1962	FLYING CLOUD	22	3050	420		19.5
1962	TRADE WIND	24 TWIN & DOUBLE	3260	400		19.5
1962	OVERLANDER	26 TWIN & DOUBLE	3720	445		19.5
1962	AMBASSADOR	28 TWIN & DOUBLE	3960	490		19.5
1962	SOVEREIGN	30 TWIN & DOUBLE	4240	580		19.5
1963	BAMBI	16	1875	200		17.5
1963	GLOBE TROTTER	19	2770	390		19.5
1963	FLYING CLOUD	22	3305	410		19.5
1963	SAFARI	22 TWIN & DOUBLE	3305	410		19.5

Year	Name	Length	Dry Wt.	Hitch Wt.	GVWR	Hitch Ball Height
1963	TRADE WIND	24 TWIN & DOUBLE	3500	415		19.5
1963	OVERLANDER	26 TWIN & DOUBLE	4095	438		19.5
1963	AMBASSADOR	28 TWIN & DOUBLE	4292	448		19.5
1963	SOVEREIGN	30 TWIN & DOUBLE	4500	490		19.5
1964	BAMBI II	17	1950	250		18.5
1964	GLOBE TROTTER	19	2890	385		19.5
1964	SAFARI	22 (SLEEP 2)	2890	385		19.5
1964	SAFARI	22 TWIN	3100	305		19.5
1964	SAFARI	22 DOUBLE	3100	305		19.5
1964	TRADE WIND	24 TWIN	3480	350		19.5
1964	TRADE WIND	24 DOUBLE	3480	350		19.5
1964	OVERLANDER	26 TWIN	3930	405		19.5
1964	OVERLANDER	26 DOUBLE	3930	405		19.5
1964	AMBASSADOR	28 TWIN	4280	420		19.5
1964	AMBASSADOR	28 DOUBLE	4280	420		19.5
1964	SOVEREIGN	30 TWIN	4500	400		19.5
1964	SOVEREIGN	30 DOUBLE	4500	400		19.5
1965	CARAVEL	17	2250	250		19.5
1965	GLOBE TROTTER	20 TWIN	2980	260		20.5
1965	GLOBE TROTTER	20 DOUBLE	2980	260		20.5
1965	SAFARI	22 TWIN	3320	350		20.5
1965	SAFARI	22 DOUBLE	3320	350		20.5
1965	TRADE WIND	24 TWIN	3810	430		20.5
1965	TRADE WIND	24 DOUBLE	3810	430		20.5
1965	OVERLANDER	26 TWIN	3950	440		20.5
1965	OVERLANDER	26 DOUBLE	3950	440		20.5
1965	AMBASSADOR	28 TWIN	4140	400		20.5
1965	AMBASSADOR	28 DOUBLE	4140	400		20.5
1965	SOVEREIGN	30 TWIN	4370	410		20.5
1965	SOVEREIGN	30 DOUBLE	4370	410		20.5
1966	CARAVEL	17	2350	250		19.5
1966	GLOBE TROTTER	20 TWIN	2910	393		20.5
1966	GLOBE TROTTER	20 DOUBLE	2910	393		20.5
1966	SAFARI	22 TWIN	3360	377		20.5
1966	SAFARI	22 DOUBLE	3360	377		20.5
1966	TRADE WIND	24 TWIN	4080	418		20.5

Year	Name	Length	Dry Wt.	Hitch Wt.	GVWR	Hitch Ball Height
1966	TRADE WIND	24 DOUBLE	4080	418		20.5
1966	OVERLANDER	26 TWIN	4250	400		20.5
1966	OVERLANDER	26 DOUBLE	4250	400		20.5
1966	AMBASSADOR	28 TWIN	4540	415		20.5
1966	AMBASSADOR	28 DOUBLE	4540	415		20.5
1966	SOVEREIGN	30 TWIN	4750	426		20.5
1966	SOVEREIGN	30 DOUBLE	4750	426		20.5
1966	CARAVEL	17	2450	300		20.5
1967	GLOBE TROTTER	20	3110	396		21.5
1967	SAFARI	22 TWIN	3450	405		21.5
1967	SAFARI	22 DOUBLE	3450	405		21.5
1967	TRADE WIND	24 TWIN	3850	440		21.5
1967	TRADE WIND	24 DOUBLE	3850	440		21.5
1967	OVERLANDER	26 TWIN	4180	450		21.5
1967	OVERLANDER	26 DOUBLE	4180	450		21.5
1967	AMBASSADOR	28 TWIN	4470	445		21.5
1967	AMBASSADOR	28 DOUBLE	4470	445		21.5
1967	SOVEREIGN	30 TWIN	4650	405		21.5
1967	SOVEREIGN	30 DOUBLE	4650	405		21.5
1968	CARAVEL	17	2460	330		17.5
1968	GLOBE TROTTER	20	2990	370		19
1968	SAFARI	22 TWIN	3490	400		19
1968	SAFARI	22 DOUBLE	3490	400		19
1968	TRADE WIND	24 TWIN	3985	445		19
1968	TRADE WIND	24 DOUBLE	3985	445		19
1968	OVERLANDER	26 TWIN	4170	435		19
1968	OVERLANDER	26 DOUBLE	4170	435		19
1968	AMBASSADOR	28 TWIN	4395	425		19
1968	AMBASSADOR	28 DOUBLE	4395	425		19
1968	SOVEREIGN	30 TWIN	4640	415		19
1968	SOVEREIGN	30 DOUBLE	4640	415		19
1969	CARAVEL SPECIAL LY	18	2880	360		19
1969	GLOBETROTTER SPECIAL LY	21	3330	390		19
1969	SAFARI DELUXE LY	23 TWIN	3860	420		19
1969	SAFARI DELUXE LY	23 DOUBLE	3860	420		19
1969	TRADE WIND DELUXE LY	25 TWIN	4340	490		19

Year	Name	Length	Dry Wt.	Hitch Wt.	GVWR	Hitch Ball Height
1969	TRADE WIND DELUXE LY	25 DOUBLE	4340	490		19
1969	OVERLANDER DELUXE LY	27 TWIN	4525	490		19
1969	OVERLANDER DELUXE LY	27 DOUBLE	4525	490		19
1969	OVERLANDER INTERNATIONAL LY	27 TWIN	4525	490		19
1969	OVERLANDER INTERNATIONAL LY	27 DOUBLE	4525	490		19
1969	AMBASSADOR INTERNATIONAL LY	29 TWIN	4715	570		19
1969	AMBASSADOR INTERNATIONAL LY	29 DOUBLE	4715	570		19
1969	SOVEREIGN INTERNATIONAL LY	31 TWIN	4995	520		19
1969	SOVEREIGN INTERNATIONAL LY	31 DOUBLE	4995	520		19
1970	CARAVEL LY	18	2880	350		19
1970	GLOBETROTTER LY	21	3330	380		19
1970	SAFARI LY	23 TWIN (BATH ON SIDE, REAR)	3500	425		19
1970	SAFARI LY	23 DOUBLE (BATH ON SIDE, REAR)	3460	415		19
1970	SAFARI LY	23 TWIN (BATH ACROSS BACK)	3850	410		19
1970	SAFARI LY	23 DOUBLE (BATH ACROSS BACK)	3800	400		19
1970	TRADE WIND DELUXE LY	25 TWIN	4250	445		19
1970	TRADE WIND DELUXE LY	25 DOUBLE	4290	455		19
1970	CARAVANNER INTERNATIONAL LY	25 (OPEN FLOOR)	4265	465		19
1970	OVERLANDER DELUXE LY	27 TWIN	4515	450		19
1970	OVERLANDER DELUXE LY	27 DOUBLE	4565	460		19
1970	OVERLANDER INTERNATIONAL LY	27 TWIN	4525	455		19
1970	OVERLANDER INTERNATIONAL LY	27 DOUBLE	4575	465		19
1970	AMBASSADOR INTERNATIONAL LY	29 TWIN	4665	445		19
1970	AMBASSADOR INTERNATIONAL LY	29 DOUBLE	4715	450		19
1970	SOVEREIGN INTERNATIONAL LY	31 TWIN	4910	480		19
1970	SOVEREIGN INTERNATIONAL LY	31 DOUBLE	4960	490		19
1971	CARAVEL LY	18	3290	360		19
1971	GLOBETROTTER LY	21	3460	420		19
1971	SAFARI LY	23 TWIN	3530	440		19
1971	SAFARI LY	23 DOUBLE	3680	445		19
1971	TRADE WIND LY	25 TWIN	4140	450		19
1971	TRADE WIND LY	25 DOUBLE	4240	455		19
1971	CARAVANNER INTERNATIONAL LY	25 (OPEN FLOOR)	4250	450		19
1971	OVERLANDER INTERNATIONAL LY	27 TWIN	4450	430		19
1971	OVERLANDER INTERNATIONAL LY	27 DOUBLE	4480	435		19
1971	AMBASSADOR INTERNATIONAL LY	29 TWIN	4650	445		19

Year	Name	Length	Dry Wt.	Hitch Wt.	GVWR	Hitch Ball Height
1971	AMBASSADOR INTERNATIONAL LY	29 DOUBLE	4690	450		19
1971	SOVEREIGN INTERNATIONAL LY	31 TWIN	4840	480		19
1971	SOVEREIGN INTERNATIONAL LY	31 DOUBLE	4910	490		19
1972	GLOBETROTTER LY	21	3380	420		19.5
1972	SAFARI LY	23 TWIN	3530	530		19.5
1972	SAFARI LY	23 DOUBLE	3570	535		19.5
1972	TRADE WIND LY	25 TWIN	4140	560		19.5
1972	TRADE WIND LY	25 DOUBLE	4220	580		19.5
1972	OVERLANDER INTERNATIONAL LY	27 TWIN	4570	540		19.5
1972	OVERLANDER INTERNATIONAL LY	27 DOUBLE	4510	480		19.5
1972	AMBASSADOR INTERNATIONAL LY	29 TWIN	4825	540		19.5
1972	AMBASSADOR INTERNATIONAL LY	29 DOUBLE	4820	510		19.5
1972	SOVEREIGN INTERNATIONAL LY	31 TWIN	4960	515		19.5
1972	SOVEREIGN INTERNATIONAL LY	31 DOUBLE	4990	520		19.5
1973	GLOBETROTTER LY	21	3380	420		19.5
1973	SAFARI LY	23 TWIN	3410	580		19.5
1973	SAFARI LY	23 DOUBLE	3450	570		19.5
1973	TRADEWIND LY	25 TWIN	4100	610		19.5
1973	TRADEWIND LY	25 DOUBLE	4180	630		19.5
1973	OVERLANDER INTERNATIONAL LY	27 TWIN	4545	515		19.5
1973	OVERLANDER INTERNATIONAL LY	27 DOUBLE	4570	500		19.5
1973	AMBASSADOR INTERNATIONAL LY	29 REAR BATH TWIN	4825	515		19.5
1973	AMBASSADOR INTERNATIONAL LY	29 REAR BATH DOUBLE	4820	485		19.5
1973	AMBASSADOR INTERNATIONAL LY	29 CENTER BATH TWIN	4740	735		19.5
1973	AMBASSADOR INTERNATIONAL LY	29 CENTER BATH DOUBLE	4710	720		19.5
1973	SOVEREIGN INTERNATIONAL LY	31 REAR BATH TWIN	5005	485		19.5
1973	SOVEREIGN INTERNATIONAL LY	31 REAR BATH DOUBLE	5035	490		19.5
1973	SOVEREIGN INTERNATIONAL LY	31 CENTER BATH TWIN	4920	695		19.5
1973	SOVEREIGN INTERNATIONAL LY	31 CENTER BATH DOUBLE	4915	730		19.5
1974	GLOBETROTTER LY	21	3390	420		19.5
1974	SAFARI LY	23 TWIN	3420	580		19.5
1974	SAFARI LY	23 DOUBLE	3460	570		19.5
1974	TRADE WIND LY	25 TWIN	4110	610		19.5
1974	TRADE WIND LY	25 DOUBLE	4190	630		19.5
1974	OVERLANDER INTERNATIONAL LY	27 TWIN	4575	515		19.5
1974	OVERLANDER INTERNATIONAL LY	27 DOUBLE	4600	500		19.5

Year	Name	Length	Dry Wt.	Hitch Wt.	GVWR	Hitch Ball Height
1974	AMBASSADOR INTERNATIONAL LY	29 REAR BATH TWIN	4855	515		19.5
1974	AMBASSADOR INTERNATIONAL LY	29 REAR BATH DOUBLE	4850	485		19.5
1974	AMBASSADOR INTERNATIONAL LY	29 CENTER BATH TWIN	4795	650		19.5
1974	AMBASSADOR INTERNATIONAL LY	29 CENTER BATH DOUBLE	4765	635		19.5
1974	SOVEREIGN INTERNATIONAL LY	31 REAR BATH TWIN	5035	490		19.5
1974	SOVEREIGN INTERNATIONAL LY	31 REAR BATH DOUBLE	5065	495		19.5
1974	SOVEREIGN INTERNATIONAL LY	31 CENTER BATH TWIN	4975	650		19.5
1974	SOVEREIGN INTERNATIONAL LY	31 CENTER BATH DOUBLE	4970	690		19.5
1975	GLOBE TROTTER LY	21	3390	420		19.5
1975	SAFARI LY	23 TWIN	3420	580		19.5
1975	SAFARI LY	23 DOUBLE	3460	570		19.5
1975	TRADE WIND LY	25 TWIN	4110	610		19.5
1975	TRADE WIND LY	25 DOUBLE	4190	630		19.5
1975	OVERLANDER INTERNATIONAL LY	27 REAR BATH TWIN	4575	515		19.5
1975	OVERLANDER INTERNATIONAL LY	27 REAR BATH DOUBLE	4600	500		19.5
1975	OVERLANDER INTERNATIONAL LY	27 CENTER BATH DOUBLE	4575	550		19.5
1975	AMBASSADOR INTERNATIONAL LY	29 REAR BATH TWIN	4855	515		19.5
1975	AMBASSADOR INTERNATIONAL LY	29 REAR BATH DOUBLE	4850	485		19.5
1975	AMBASSADOR INTERNATIONAL LY	29 CENTER BATH TWIN	4795	650		19.5
1975	AMBASSADOR INTERNATIONAL LY	29 CENTER BATH DOUBLE	4765	635		19.5
1975	SOVEREIGN INTERNATIONAL LY	31 REAR BATH TWIN	5035	490		19.5
1975	SOVEREIGN INTERNATIONAL LY	31 REAR BATH DOUBLE	5065	495		19.5
1975	SOVEREIGN INTERNATIONAL LY	31 CENTER BATH TWIN	4975	650		19.5
1975	SOVEREIGN INTERNATIONAL LY	31 CENTER BATH DOUBLE	4970	690		19.5
1976	GLOBE TROTTER LY	21	3390	420		19.5
1976	SAFARI LY	23 TWIN	3420	580		19.5
1976	SAFARI LY	23 DOUBLE	3460	570		19.5
1976	TRADE WIND LY	25 TWIN	4110	610		19.5
1976	TRADE WIND LY	25 DOUBLE	4190	630		19.5
1976	OVERLANDER INTERNATIONAL LY	27 REAR BATH TWIN	4575	515		19.5
1976	OVERLANDER INTERNATIONAL LY	27 REAR BATH DOUBLE	4600	500		19.5
1976	OVERLANDER INTERNATIONAL LY	27 CENTER BATH DOUBLE	4575	550		19.5
1976	AMBASSADOR INTERNATIONAL LY	29 REAR BATH TWIN	4855	515		19.5
1976	AMBASSADOR INTERNATIONAL LY	29 REAR BATH DOUBLE	4850	485		19.5
1976	AMBASSADOR INTERNATIONAL LY	29 CENTER BATH TWIN	4795	650		19.5
1976	AMBASSADOR INTERNATIONAL LY	29 CENTER BATH DOUBLE	4765	635		19.5

Year	Name	Length	Dry Wt.	Hitch Wt.	GVWR	Hitch Ball Height
1976	SOVEREIGN INTERNATIONAL LY	31 REAR BATH TWIN	5035	490		19.5
1976	SOVEREIGN INTERNATIONAL LY	31 REAR BATH DOUBLE	5065	495		19.5
1976	SOVEREIGN INTERNATIONAL LY	31 CENTER BATH TWIN	4975	650		19.5
1976	SOVEREIGN INTERNATIONAL LY	31 CENTER BATH DOUBLE	4970	690		19.5
1977	GLOBE TROTTER LY	21	3410	490		19.5
1977	SAFARI LY	23 DOUBLE	3850	745		19.5
1977	SAFARI LY	23 TWIN	3800	750		19.5
1977	TRADE WIND LY	25 TWIN	4090	725		19.5
1977	TRADE WIND LY	25 DOUBLE	4175	735		19.5
1977	CARAVANNER LY	25 (OPEN FLOOR MODEL)	4435	580		19.5
1977	OVERLANDER LY	27 TWIN	4520	590		19.5
1977	OVERLANDER LY	27 DOUBLE	4550	570		19.5
1977	AMBASSADOR LY	29 REAR BATH TWIN	4830	605		19.5
1977	AMBASSADOR LY	29 REAR BATH DOUBLE	4840	590		19.5
1977	AMBASSADOR LY	29 CENTER BATH TWIN	4790	720		19.5
1977	AMBASSADOR LY	29 CENTER BATH DOUBLE	4775	725		19.5
1977	SOVEREIGN LY	31 REAR BATH TWIN	5040	630		19.5
1977	SOVEREIGN LY	31 REAR BATH DOUBLE	5070	620		19.5
1977	SOVEREIGN LY	31 CENTER BATH TWIN	5025	710		19.5
1977	SOVEREIGN LY	31 CENTER BATH DOUBLE	5005	715		19.5
1978	SAFARI	23	3905	500		19.5
1978	CARAVANNER	25 (SALON MODEL)	4380	580		19.5
1978	TRADE WIND	25 TWIN	4005	670		19.5
1978	TRADE WIND	25 DOUBLE	3975	610		19.5
1978	AMBASSADOR	28 TWIN	4630	550		19.5
1978	AMBASSADOR	28 DOUBLE	4690	575		19.5
1978	SOVEREIGN	31 REAR BATH WIN	4780	555		19.5
1978	SOVEREIGN	31 REAR BATH DOUBLE	4850	580		19.5
1978	SOVEREIGN	31 CENTER BATH TWIN	4810	545		19.5
1978	SOVEREIGN	31 CENTER	4800	545		19.5
1979	SAFARI	23 BATH DOUBLE	3905	500		19.5
1979	TRADE WIND	25 DOUBLE	3975	610		19.5
1979	TRADE WIND	25 TWIN	4005	670		19.5
1979	AMBASSADOR	28 DOUBLE	4690	575		19.5
1979	AMBASSADOR	28 TWIN	4630	550		19.5
1979	SOVEREIGN	31 CENTER BATH DOUBLE	4800	545		19.5

Year	Name	Length	Dry Wt.	Hitch Wt.	GVWR	Hitch Ball Height
1979	SOVEREIGN	31 CENTER BATH TWIN	4810	545		19.5
1979	SOVEREIGN	31 REAR BATH DOUBLE	4850	580		19.5
1979	SOVEREIGN	31 REAR BATH TWIN	4780	555		19.5
1980	CARAVELLE	20 DOUBLE	2539	309		19.5
1980	CARAVELLE	22 DOUBLE	2799	249		19.5
1980	CARAVELLE	24 TWIN & DOUBLE	3317	347		19.5
1980	INTERNATIONAL	25 DOUBLE	3926	554		19.5
1980	INTERNATIONAL	25 TWIN	3956	614		19.5
1980	INTERNATIONAL	28 DOUBLE	4200	597		19.5
1980	INTERNATIONAL	28 TWIN	4143	571		19.5
1980	INTERNATIONAL	31 REAR BATH DOUBLE	4552	597		19.5
1980	INTERNATIONAL	31 REAR BATH TWIN	4485	571		19.5
1980	INTERNATIONAL	31 CENTER BATH DOUBLE	4603	583		19.5
1980	INTERNATIONAL	31 REAR BATH TWIN	4612	583		19.5
1980	EXCELLA II	25 TWIN	4244	669		19.5
1980	EXCELLA II	25 DOUBLE	4212	604		19.5
1980	EXCELLA II	28 TWIN	4443	622		19.5
1980	EXCELLA II	28 DOUBLE	4504	650		19.5
1980	EXCELLA II	31 REAR BATH TWIN	4691	622		19.5
1980	EXCELLA II	31 REAR BATH DOUBLE	4762	650		19.5
1980	EXCELLA II	31 CENTER BATH TWIN	4795	606		19.5
1980	EXCELLA II	31 CENTER BATH DOUBLE	4785	606		19.5
1981	INTERNATIONAL & EXCELLA II	20	2700	360		14.75
1981	INTERNATIONAL & EXCELLA II	22	3200	350		
1981	INTERNATIONAL & EXCELLA II	24	3300	400		14.75
1981	INTERNATIONAL & EXCELLA II	25	3600	475		16.75
1981	INTERNATIONAL & EXCELLA II	27	4230	490		18.75
1981	INTERNATIONAL & EXCELLA II	31 T/D (REAR BATH)	4630	600		18.75
1981	INTERNATIONAL & EXCELLA II	31 A/B (CENTER BATH) A=T B=D	4680	580		18.75
1981	EXCELLA LIMITED	27	4980	700		18.75
1981	EXCELLA LIMITED	31 T/D (REAR BATH)	5500	720		18.75
1981	EXCELLA LIMITED	31 A/B (CENTER BATH) A=T B=D	5550	725		18.75
1982	INTERNATIONAL	27 REAR BATH	6000	490		18.75
1982	INTERNATIONAL	31 SIDE BATH	6800	580		18.75
1982	INTERNATIONAL	31 REAR BATH	6800	600		18.75
1982	EXCELLA	27 REAR BATH	6000	590		18.75

Year	Name	Length	Dry Wt.	Hitch Wt.	GVWR	Hitch Ball Height
1982	EXCELLA	31 SIDE BATH	6800	600		18.75
1982	EXCELLA	31 REAR BATH	6800	650		18.75
1982	EXCELLA	34 SIDE BATH	8300	700		18.75
1982	LIMITED	31 SIDE BATH	8300	725		18.75
1982	LIMITED	31 REAR BATH	8300	720		18.75
1982	LIMITED	34 SIDE BATH	8900	770		18.75
1983	INTERNATIONAL	27 REAR BATH	4230	490		18.75
1983	INTERNATIONAL	31 REAR BATH	4630	600		18.75
1983	INTERNATIONAL	31 CENTER BATH	4680	580		18.75
1983	EXCELLA	27 REAR BATH	4500	590		18.75
1983	EXCELLA	31 REAR BATH	4900	650		18.75
1983	EXCELLA	31 CENTER BATH	4950	600		18.75
1983	EXCELLA	34 REAR BATH	5800	600		18.75
1983	EXCELLA	34 CENTER BATH	5500	700		18.75
1983	LIMITED	31 REAR BATH	5500	720		18.75
1983	LIMITED	31 CENTER BATH	5550	725		18.75
1983	LIMITED	34 REAR BATH	6600	800		18.75
1983	LIMITED	34 CENTER BATH	6400	770		18.75
1984	SOVEREIGN	27 REAR BATH	4820	550		18.75
1984	SOVEREIGN	29 CENTER BATH	5300	550		18.75
1984	SOVEREIGN	31 CENTER BATH	5400	575		18.75
1984	INTERNATIONAL	31 REAR & CENTER BATH	5600	650		18.75
1984	INTERNATIONAL	34 REAR & CENTER BATH	6250	630		18.75
1984	EXCELLA	31 REAR & CENTER BATH	5650	600		18.75
1984	EXCELLA	34 REAR & CENTER BATH	6350	640		18.75
1984	LIMITED	31 REAR & CENTER BATH	6250	650		18.75
1984	LIMITED	34 REAR & CENTER BATH	6950	700		18.75
1985	SOVEREIGN	25 SIDE BATH	4900	755		18.75
1985	SOVEREIGN	27 REAR BATH	4950	650		18.75
1985	SOVEREIGN	29 SIDE BATH	5300	620		18.75
1985	SOVEREIGN	31 SIDE & REAR BATH	5600	590		18.75
1985	SOVEREIGN	34 SIDE & REAR BATH	6600	710		18.75
1985	EXCELLA	31 SIDE & REAR BATH	5800	690		18.75
1985	EXCELLA	34 SIDE & REAR BATH	6800	680		18.75
1985	LIMITED	31 SIDE BATH	6200	780		18.75
1985	LIMITED	34 SIDE BATH	7200	760		18.75

Year	Name	Length	Dry Wt.	Hitch Wt.	GVWR	Hitch Ball Height
1986	ARGOSY	32 TWIN & DOUBLE	5600	600		
1986	ARGOSY	29 TWIN & DOUBLE	5390	580		
1986	ARGOSY	33 FRONT KITCHEN, TWIN & DOUBLE	6235	685		
1986	SOVEREIGN	25 SIDE BATH	4900	755		18.75
1986	SOVEREIGN	27 REAR BATH	4950	650		18.75
1986	SOVEREIGN	29 SIDE BATH	5300	620		18.75
1986	SOVEREIGN	31 SIDE BATH	5600	590		18.75
1986	EXCELLA	32 SIDE BATH	6440	820		18.75
1986	EXCELLA	34 SIDE BATH	7040	810		18.75
1986	LIMITED	32 SIDE BATH	6840	850		18.75
1986	LIMITED	34 SIDE BATH	7440	840		18.75
1987	SOVEREIGN	23	4300	520		18.75
1987	SOVEREIGN	25 SIDE BATH	5100	700		18.75
1987	SOVEREIGN	27 REAR BATH	5000	650		18.75
1987	SOVEREIGN	29 SIDE BATH	5300	700		18.75
1987	EXCELLA	31 SIDE BATH	5900	700		18.75
1987	EXCELLA	32 SIDE BATH (W/O DINETTE)	6300	800		18.75
1987	EXCELLA	32 SIDE BATH (WITH DINETTE)	6500	800		18.75
1987	EXCELLA	34 SIDE BATH	7100	800		18.75
1987	LIMITED	32 SIDE BATH	6900	850		18.75
1987	LIMITED	34 SIDE BATH	7500	850		18.75
1987	ARGOSY	27 TWIN & DOUBLE	5100	550		
1987	ARGOSY	29 TWIN & DOUBLE	5400	600		
1987	ARGOSY	32 TWIN & DOUBLE (REAR DOOR OPT)	5600	600		
1988	EXCELLA	23	4300	520		
1988	EXCELLA	25	5100	700		
1988	EXCELLA	27	5200	650		
1988	EXCELLA	29	5600	700		
1988	EXCELLA	32 W/DINETTE	6500	800		
1988	EXCELLA	32W/O DINETTE	6300	700		
1988	EXCELLA	32WTB	6200	700		
1988	EXCELLA	34W/DINETTE	7100	800		
1988	EXCELLA	34WTB	6700	740		
1988	LIMITED	34WTB	7025	800		
1989	EXCELLA	25	5100	700		18.75
1989	EXCELLA	29	5600	700		18.75

Year	Name	Length	Dry Wt.	Hitch Wt.	GVWR	Hitch Ball Height
1989	EXCELLA	32W/DINETTE	6500	800		18.75
1989	EXCELLA	32W/O DINETTE	6300	700		18.75
1989	EXCELLA	34WTB	6700	740		18.75
1989	EXCELLA	34 W/DINETTE	7100	800		18.75
1989	LIMITED	34WTB	7025	800		18.75
1989	LIMITED	34W/DINETTE	7400	800		18.75
1989	LAND YACHT	29	5550	600	7300	18
1989	LAND YACHT	32	5800	600	7300	18
1989	LAND YACHT	33	6300	700	8500	18
1989	LAND YACHT	35	6500	700	8900	18
1989	LAND YACHT	5TH WHEEL	9100	2000	11000	N/A
1990	LAND YACHT	29	5800	600	7300	18
1990	LAND YACHT	32	6000	600	7300	18
1990	LAND YACHT	33	6500	800	8500	18
1990	LAND YACHT	35	6700	700	8900	18
1990	EXCELLA	25	5100	700		18.75
1990	EXCELLA	29	5600	700		18.75
1990	EXCELLA	32 W/DINETTE	6500	800		18.75
1990	EXCELLA	32W/DINETTE	6300	700		18.75
1990	EXCELLA	32RB	6350	700		18.75
1990	EXCELLA	34	7100	800		18.75
1990	LIMITED	34	7100	800		18.75
1991	EXCELLA	25	5100	700		1'6-3/4 "
1991	EXCELLA	29	5600	700		1'6-3/4 "
1991	EXCELLA	32W/O DINETTE	6300	700		1'6-3/4 "
1991	EXCELLA	32RB	6350	700		1'6-3/4 "
1991	EXCELLA	34	6900	800		1'6-3/4 "
1991	LIMITED	34	7300	800		1'6-3/4 "
1992	SOVEREIGN	21	3900	550	5500	1'6-3/4 "
1992	EXCELLA	25	5100	700	6800	1'6-3/4 "
1992	EXCELLA	29	5600	700	6800	1'6-3/4 "
1992	EXCELLA	32W/DINETTE	6500	800	8300	1'6-3/4 "
1992	EXCELLA	32W/O DINETTE	6300	700	8300	1'6-3/4 "

Year	Name	Length	Dry Wt.	Hitch Wt.	GVWR	Hitch Ball Height
1992	EXCELLA	34WTB	6700	740	8900	1'6-3/4"
1992	EXCELLA	34W/DINETTE	7100	800	8900	1'6-3/4"
1992	LIMITED	34WTB	7025	800	8850	1'6-3/4"
1992	LIMITED	34W/DINETTE	7400	800	8900	1'6-3/4"
1993	SOVEREIGN	21	3900	550		
1993	EXCELLA	25	5100	700		
1993	EXCELLA	29	5600	700		
1993	EXCELLA	30	6350	750		
1993	EXCELLA	32W/O DINETTE	6300	700		
1993	EXCELLA	32RB	6350	700		
1993	EXCELLA	34	7100	800		
1993	LIMITED	34	7400	800		
1994	EXCELLA	25	5100	700	6800	
1994	EXCELLA	28	6100	620	8200	
1994	EXCELLA	30	6350	750	8300	
1994	EXCELLA	34	7100	800	8900	
1994	LIMITED	30	6350	750	8300	
1994	LIMITED	34	7100	800	8900	
1995	SOVEREIGN	21	3900	550	5500	
1995	EXCELLA	25	5100	700	6800	
1995	EXCELLA	28	6100	620	8200	
1995	EXCELLA	30	6350	750	8300	
1995	EXCELLA	34	7100	800	8900	
1995	EXCELLA	34FK	7700	825	9500	
1995	LIMITED	30	6350	750	8300	
1995	LIMITED	34	7100	800	8900	
1995	LIMITED	34FK	7700	825	9500	
1996	CUTTER FORD	30	13780		17000	
1996	CUTTER CHEVY	30	NA		16500	
1996	CUTTER PUSHER FREIGHTLINER	32	15310		19840	
1996	CUTTER FORD	34	15140		20000	
1996	CUTTER CHEVY	34	14835		19500	

Year	Name	Length	Dry Wt.	Hitch Wt.	GVWR	Hitch Ball Height
1996	CUTTER SLIDE FORD	34	15550		20000	
1996	CUTTER FORD	36	15950		20000	
1996	CUTTER CHEVY	36	NA		19500	
1996	LAND YACHT CHEVY	30	13240		16500	
1996	LAND YACHT CHEVY	33	13900		16500	
1996	LAND YACHT FREIGHTLINER	35WB	18940		21500	
1996	SOVEREIGN	21	4265	600	5500	1' 5-3/4 "
1996	EXCELLA	25	6000	730	7300	1' 6-3/4 "
1996	EXCELLA	28	6720	680	8200	1' 6-3/4 "
1996	EXCELLA	30	6855	670	8300	1' 6-3/4 "
1996	EXCELLA	34	7855	800	9500	1' 6-3/4 "
1996	EXCELLA	34FK	8140	900	9500	1' 6-3/4 "
1996	LIMITED	30	7050	750	8300	1' 6-3/4 "
1996	LIMITED	34	8530	800	9500	1' 6-3/4 "
1996	LIMITED	34FK	8320	825	9500	1' 6-3/4 "
1997	EXCELLA	21RB	4760	560	6200	
1997	EXCELLA	25SB	5840	760	7300	
1997	EXCELLA	28SB	6580	630	8200	
1997	EXCELLA	30SB	6810	610	8300	
1997	LIMITED	30SB	6940	760	8300	
1997	LIMITED	34FK	7840	710	9800	
1997	LIMITED	34FK	8080	770	9800	
1997	EXCELLA	34SB	7710	820	9800	
1997	LIMITED	34SB	7950	870	9800	
1997	SAFARI	25	4690	680	5500	
1997	LAND YACHT CHEVY	30			16500	
1997	LAND YACHT CHEVY	33			16500	
1997	LAND YACHT FREIGHTLINER	35			23000	
1997	CUTTER CHEVY	30			16500	
1997	CUTTER FORD	30			17000	
1997	CUTTER FREIGHTLINER	32			20500	
1997	CUTTER CHEVY	34			19500	
1997	CUTTER FORD	34			20000	
1997	CUTTER SLIDE FORD	34			20000	
1997	CUTTER FREIGHTLINER	35			24350	

Year	Name	Length	Dry Wt.	Hitch Wt.	GVWR	Hitch Ball Height
1997	LAND YACHT CHEVY	30			16500	
1997	LAND YACHT CHEVY	33			16500	
1997	LAND YACHT FREIGHTLINER	35			23000	
1997	CUTTER CHEVY	30			16500	
1997	CUTTER FORD	30			17000	
1997	CUTTER FREIGHTLINER	32			20500	
1997	CUTTER CHEVY	34			19500	
1997	CUTTER FORD	34			20000	
1997	CUTTER FORD	34S			20000	
1997	CUTTER FREIGHTLINER	35			24350	
1998	BAMBI	19	3530	430		15 3/4
1998	SAFARI	25C	4750	680	6300	
1998	SAFARI	25A	4900	680	6300	
1998	SAFARI	25B	4850	680	6300	
1998	EXCELLA	25	5840	760	7300	1'6-3/4 "
1998	EXCELLA	28	6850	630	8200	1'6-3/4 "
1998	EXCELLA 1000	30	6810	610	8300	1'6-3/4 "
1998	EXCELLA 1000	31	7000	690	8300	1'6-3/4 "
1998	EXCELLA 1000	34	7710	820	9800	1'6-3/4 "
1998	EXCELLA 1000	34FK	7840	710	9800	1'6-3/4 "
1998	LIMITED	30	6940	760	8300	1'6-3/4 "
1998	LIMITED	31	6940	760	8300	1'6-3/4 "
1998	LIMITED	34	7950	870	9800	1'6-3/4 "
1998	LIMITED	34FK	8080	770	9800	1'6-3/4 "
1998	LAND YACHT GAS CHEVY	30	13650		16500	
1998	LAND YACHT GAS CHEVY	33	14120		16500	
1998	LAND YACHT WB DIESEL FREIGHTLINER	35	18650		24590	
1998	CUTTER CHEVY	30	14270		16500	
1998	CUTTER CHEVY	34	15580		19500	
1998	CUTTER DIESEL FREIGHTLINER	35	19580		26350	
1998	CUTTER DIESEL SLIDE FREIGHTLINER	35	20470		26350	
1999	EXCELLA	34	8070	820	9800	
1999	LIMITED	34	8290	870	9800	
1999	EXCELLA	34FK	8170	710	9800	
1999	LIMITED	34FK	8420	770	9800	

Year	Name	Length	Dry Wt.	Hitch Wt.	GVWR	Hitch Ball Height
1999	EXCELLA	34S/O			10500	
1999	LIMITED	34S/O			10500	
1999	LAND YACHT	30	13650		16500	
1999	LAND YACHT	33	14170		16500	
1999	LAND YACHT	35WB	19400		24590	
1999	CUTTER CHEVY	30	14320		16500	
1999	CUTTER CHEVY	34	15630		19500	
1999	CUTTER W/ SLIDE	34C	17000		19500	
1999	CUTTER	35P	20462		26350	
1999	CUTTER W/SLIDE	35P	21562		26350	
2000	BAMBI	19	3600	500	4500	
2000	SAFARI	23	4700	500	6300	
2000	SAFARI	25	4920	680	6300	
2000	SAFARI SS	25	4770	680	6300	
2000	SAFARI	27	5440	730	7300	
2000	EXCELLA	25	6000	760	7300	
2000	EXCELLA	28	6730	630	8200	
2000	EXCELLA	30	7180	760	8300	
2000	LIMITED	30	7300	760	8300	
2000	EXCELLA	31	7150	690	8300	
2000	LIMITED	31	7270	760	8300	
2000	EXCELLA	34	8070	820	9800	
2000	LIMITED	34	8290	870	9800	
2000	LIMITED S/O	34	9050	1250	10500	
2000	LIMITED S/O CSA	34	9050	1250	11500	
2000	LAND YACHT	30	13650		16500	
2000	LAND YACHT	33	14170		16500	
2000	XC W/SLIDE	35	21562		26350	
2000	35SXL DBL SLIDE	35	18300		20500	
2000	350XL SGL SLIDE	35	18175		20500	
2000	390XL	39	24450		29410	
2001	BAMBI	19	3600	500	4500	17.25 "
2001	SAFARI	23	4700	500	6300	18.75 "
2001	SAFARI	25	4920	680	6300	18.75 "

Year	Name	Length	Dry Wt.	Hitch Wt.	GVWR	Hitch Ball Height
2001	SAFARI SS	25	4770	680	6300	18.75 "
2001	SAFARI	27	5440	730	7300	18.75 "
2001	EXCELLA	25	6000	760	7300	18.75 "
2001	EXCELLA	28	6730	630	8200	18.75 "
2001	EXCELLA	30	7180	760	8300	18.75 "
2001	LIMITED	30	7300	760	8300	18.75 "
2001	EXCELLA	31	7150	690	8300	18.75 "
2001	LIMITED	31	7270	760	8300	18.75 "
2001	EXCELLA	34	8070	820	9800	18.75 "
2001	LIMITED	34	8290	870	9800	18.75 "
2001	EXCELLA S/O	34	9110	1250	10,500	19.75"
2001	EXCELLA S/O CSA	34	9110	1250	11,500	19.75"
2001	LIMITED S/O	34	9050	1250	10500	19.75"
2001	LIMITED S/O CSA	34	9050	1250	11500	19.75"
2001	LAND YACHT	30	14150		18000	
2001	LAND YACHT	33	14170		16500	
2001	XC360	36	22950		26350	
2001	355XL DBL SLIDE	35	18300		20500	
2001	350XL SGL SLIDE	35	18175		20500	
2001	390XL	39	24800		29410	
2001	395XL	39	25750		29410	
2002	BAMBI	16	2855	325	3500	18.00 "
2002	BAMBI	19	3600	500	4500	17.25 "
2002	SAFARI	23	4700	500	6300	17.75 "
2002	SAFARI	25A	4920	680	6300	17.75 "
2002	SAFARI	25B	4850	680	6300	17.75 "
2002	SAFARI	25 SIX SLEEPER	4770	680	6300	17.75 "
2002	SAFARI	27A	5440	730	7300	17.75 "
2002	SAFARI	27B	5390	730	7300	17.75 "
2002	CLASSIC	25	6000	760	7300	18.75 "
2002	CLASSIC	28	6730	630	8600	18.75 "
2002	CLASSIC	30	7180	760	8700	18.75 "
2002	CLASSIC SLIDE-OUT	30	7900	900	9100	19.75 "
2002	CLASSIC SLIDE-OUT CSA	30	7900	900	10,000	19.75 "
2002	CLASSIC	31	7150	690	8700	18.75 "
2002	CLASSIC	34	8070	820	9800	18.75 "

Year	Name	Length	Dry Wt.	Hitch Wt.	GVWR	Hitch Ball Height
2002	CLASSIC SLIDE-OUT SOFA	34	9110	1250	10,500	19.75 "
2002	CLASSIC SLIDE-OUT DINETTE	34	9110	1050	10,500	19.75 "
2002	CLASSIC SLIDE-OUT CSA	34	9110	1250	11,500	19.75 "
2002	INTERNATIONAL 22 AS	22	4290	600	5000	18"
2002	INTERNATIONAL 22CCD	22	4000	400	5300	18"
2002	LAND YACHT	26	12,524		15,000	
2002	LAND YACHT	30	14,150		18,000	
2002	LAND YACHT	33	14,670		18,000	
2002	XC360	36	22,950		26,850	
2002	XC365	36	23,600		26,850	
2002	XL390	39	24,800		31,000	
2002	XL395	39	25,750		31,000	
2002	XL396	39	25,750		31,000	
2003	BAMBI	19	3770	425	4500	17.25 "
2003	SAFARI	25 SIX SLEEPER	5220	750	6300	17.75 "
2003	SAFARI	25A	4920	680	6300	17.75 "
2003	SAFARI	25B	4920	680	6300	17.75 "
2003	CLASSIC	25	6050	870	7300	18.75 "
2003	CLASSIC	28	6760	800	8600	18.75 "
2003	CLASSIC	30	7230	730	8700	18.75 "
2003	CLASSIC SLIDE-OUT	30	8000	1080	9100	19.75 "
2003	CLASSIC SLIDE-OUT CSA	30	8000	1080	10,000	19.75 "
2003	CLASSIC	31	7200	700	8700	18.75 "
2003	CLASSIC	34	8070	820	9800	18.75 "
2003	CLASSIC SLIDE-OUT SOFA	34	8760	1250	10,500	19.75 "
2003	CLASSIC SLIDE-OUT DINETTE	34	8890	1240	10,500	19.75 "
2003	CLASSIC SLIDE-OUT SOFA CSA	34	8760	1250	11,500	19.75 "
2003	CLASSIC SLIDE-OUT DINETTE CSA	34	8890	1240	11,500	19.75 "
2003	INTERNATIONAL 22 AS	22	4290	600	5000	18"
2003	INTERNATIONAL 22 CCD	22	4210	600	5000	18"
2003	LAND YACHT	26	12,524		15,000	
2003	LAND YACHT	30	14,540		18,000	
2003	LAND YACHT	33	15,070		18,000	
2003	XC360	36	22,950		26,850	
2003	XC365	36	23,600		26,850	

Year	Name	Length	Dry Wt.	Hitch Wt.	GVWR	Hitch Ball Height
2003	XL390	39	25,245		*41,000	
2003	XL395	39	25,750		*41,000	
2003	XL396	39	25,750		*41,000	
	*Due to chassis units before S/N 810839 in the 2003 model year 390XL have GVWR of 36,000 lbs.					
2004	Safari	19	3600	500	4500	17 1/4"
2004	Safari	22	4190	510	5600	18"
2004	Safari	25	4920	680	6300	17 3/4"
2004	Safari SS	25	5270	750	6300	17 3/4"
2004	Safari	28	5580	890	7300	17 3/4"
2004	Safari S/O	28	6680	1250	9100	17 3/4"
2004	International CCD	16	2785	375	3500	18"
2004	International CCD	19	3715	460	4500	17 1/4"
2004	International CCD	22	4043	590	5600	18"
2004	International CCD	25	5220	740	6300	17 3/4"
2004	International CCD	28	5460	900	7300	17 3/4"
2004	Classic	25	6050	870	7300	18 3/4"
2004	Classic	28	6785	730	8600	18 3/4"
2004	Classic	30	7230	730	8700	18 3/4"
2004	Classic	31	7880	890	8700	18 3/4"
2004	Classic	34	8070	820	9800	18 3/4"
2004	Classic S/O	30	7877	1125	9100	18 3/4"
2004	Classic S/O Lounge	34	8760	1490	10500	18 3/4"
2004	Classic S/O Dinette	34	9022	1250	10500	18 3/4"
2004	Land Yacht Motorhome	26	12700	N/A	15000	N/A

Year	Name	Length	Dry Wt.	Hitch Wt.	GVWR	Hitch Ball Height
2004	Land Yacht Motorhome	30	14503	N/A	18000	N/A
2004	Land Yacht Motorhome S/O	30	14942	N/A	18000	N/A
2004	Land Yacht Motorhome	33	15023	N/A	18000	N/A
2004	Land Yacht 390 XL Pusher Motorhome	39	25058	N/A	31000	N/A
2004	Land Yacht 396 XL Pusher Motorhome	39	26377	N/A	31000	N/A
2004	390 XL Skydeck Motorhome	39	26357	N/A	31000	N/A
2004	Interstate	22	6580	N/A	8550	N/A
2005	Safari	16			3500	18"
2005	Safari	19	3600	440	4500	17 1/4"
2005	Safari	22	4190	500	5600	18"
2005	Safari	25	4920	510	6300	17 3/4"
2005	Safari SS	25	5270	680	6300	17 3/4"
2005	Safari FB	25	5580	750	6300	17 3/4"
2005	Safari	28	6680	890	7300	17 3/4"
2005	Safari S/O	28	6215	1250	9100	17 3/4"
2005	Safari	30		850	8400	17 3/4"
2005	International CCD	16	2785	375	3500	18"
2005	International CCD	19	3715	460	4500	17 1/4"
2005	International CCD	22	4043	590	5600	18"
2005	International CCD	25	5220	740	6300	17 3/4"
2005	International CCD	28	5460	900	7300	17 3/4"
2005	Classic	25	6050	870	8000	18 3/4"
2005	Classic	28	6785	730	9000	18 3/4"
2005	Classic	30	7230	730	10000	18 3/4"
2005	Classic S/O	30	7877	1125	10300	19 3/4"
2005	Classic D	31	7880	890	10000	18 3/4"
2005	Classic	34	8070	820	11500	18 3/4"
2005	Classic S/O	34	9022	1250	11500	19 3/4"
2005	Land Yacht Motorhome	26	12700	N/A	15000	N/A
2005	Land Yacht Motorhome	30	14503	N/A	18000	N/A
2005	Land Yacht Motorhome S/O	30	14942	N/A	18000	N/A
2005	Land Yacht Motorhome	33	15023	N/A	18000	N/A
2005	Land Yacht 390 XL Pusher Motorhome	39	25058	N/A	31000	N/A
2005	Land Yacht 396 XL Pusher Motorhome	39	26377	N/A	31000	N/A

Year	Name	Length	Dry Wt.	Hitch Wt.	GVWR	Hitch Ball Height
2005	390 XL Skydeck Motorhome	39	26357	N/A	31000	N/A
2005	A37 Motorhome	37	26760	N/A	32000	N/A
2005	Interstate	22	6453	N/A	8550	N/A
2005	Interstate Mid Bath	22	6580	N/A	8550	N/A
2005	Westfalia	18	7100	N/A	8550	N/A
2006	Safari	16	2950	390	3500	18"
2006	Safari	19	3680	480	4500	17 3/4"
2006	Safari	20	3965		5000	17 3/4"
2006	Safari	22	4160	510	5600	18"
2006	Safari	23	4500	600	6000	18"
2006	Safari	25	5065	860	7000	17 3/4"
2006	Safari SS	25	5380	750	7300	17 3/4"
2006	Safari FB	25	5210	720	7300	17 3/4"
2006	Safari	28	5495	830	7300	17 3/4"
2006	Safari S/O	28	6515	1010	9100	17 3/4"
2006	Safari	30	6215	850	8400	17 3/4"
2006	International CCD	16	2825	430	3500	18"
2006	International CCD	19	3575	510	4500	17 1/4"
2006	International CCD	22	4105	460	5600	18"
2006	International CCD	25	5145	740	7000	17 3/4"
2006	International CCD	28	5440	880	7300	17 3/4"
2006	Classic	25	5900	870	8000	18 3/4"
2006	Classic	28	6570	890	9000	18 3/4"
2006	Classic	30	7095	670	10000	18 3/4"
2006	Classic S/O	30	7900	1050	10300	19 3/4"
2006	Classic	31	7030	770	10000	18 3/4"
2006	Classic D	31	6990	760	10000	18 3/4"
2006	Classic	34	7910	790	11500	18 3/4"
2006	Classic S/O	34	9022	1250	11500	19 3/4"
2006	Land Yacht Motorhome	26	12700	N/A	15000	N/A
2006	Land Yacht Motorhome	30	14503	N/A	18000	N/A
2006	Land Yacht Motorhome S/O	30	14942	N/A	18000	N/A
2006	Land Yacht Motorhome	33	15023	N/A	18000	N/A
2006	Land Yacht 390 XL Pusher Motohrome	39	25058	N/A	32000	N/A
2006	Land Yacht 396 XL Pusher Motorhome	39	23703	N/A	32000	N/A

Year	Name	Length	Dry Wt.	Hitch Wt.	GVWR	Hitch Ball Height
2006	390 XL Skydeck Motorhome	39	26357	N/A	32000	N/A
2006	390 XL Skydeck Bunk Motorhome	39	26357	N/A	32000	N/A
2006	A37 Motorhome	37	26760	N/A	32000	N/A
2006	A39 Motorhome	39	27574	N/A	32000	N/A
2006	Parkway	22	6408	N/A	8550	N/A
2006	Parkway Mid Bath	22		N/A	8550	N/A
2006	Interstate	22	6453	N/A	8550	N/A
2006	Interstate Mid Bath	22	6740	N/A	8550	N/A
2007	75th Anniversary	19	3625	530	4500	17 1/4"
2007	BaseCamp	16	1965	350	3250	18"
2007	Safari	19	3680	480	4500	17 3/4"
2007	Safari	20	3965	600	5000	17 3/4"
2007	Safari	23	4460	600	6000	17 3/4"
2007	Safari	25	5065	860	7000	17 3/4"
2007	Safari SS	25	5380	750	7300	17 3/4"
2007	Safari FB	25	5210	720	7300	17 3/4"
2007	Safari	27	5399	790	7600	17 3/4"
2007	Safari	28	5495	830	7300	17 3/4"
2007	International CCD	16	2825	430	3500	18"
2007	International CCD	19	3575	510	4500	17 1/4"
2007	International CCD	23	4580	700	6000	17 3/4"
2007	International CCD	25	5145	740	7000	17 3/4"
2007	International CCD	25	5382	780	7300	17 3/4"
2007	International CCD	27	5813	790	7600	17 3/4"
2007	International CCD	28	5440	880	7300	18 3/4"
2007	Classic	25	6074	870	8000	18 3/4"
2007	Classic FB	25	5900	780	8000	18 3/4"
2007	Classic	27	6525	790	9000	18 3/4"
2007	Classic	28	6590	890	9000	18 3/4"
2007	Classic	30	7095	670	10000	18 3/4"
2007	Classic S/O	30	2360	1050	10300	18 3/4"
2007	Classic	31	7030	770	10000	18 3/4"
2007	Classic D	31	7050	760	10000	18 3/4"
2007	Classic	34	7858	770	11500	18 3/4"
2007	Classic S/O	34	8247	1150	11500	18 3/4"

Year	Name	Length	Dry Wt.	Hitch Wt.	GVWR	Hitch Ball Height
2007	Interstate	22	6453	N/A	8550	N/A
2007	Interstate Mid Bath	22	6475	N/A	8550	N/A
2007	Land Yacht 396 XL Pusher Motorhome	39	23703	N/A	32000	N/A
2008	Safari Sport	17	2800	300	3500	16 1/2"
2008	Safari Sport	22	3350	370	4000	17 1/4"
2008	Safari	19	3680	480	4500	17 3/4"
2008	Safari	20	3965	600	5000	17 3/4"
2008	Safari	23	4460	600	6000	17 3/4"
2008	Safari	25	5065	860	7000	17 3/4"
2008	Safari SS	25	5380	750	7300	17 3/4"
2008	Safari FB	25	5210	720	7300	17 3/4"
2008	Safari	27	5399	790	7600	17 3/4"
2008	Safari	28	5495	830	7300	17 3/4"
2008	Safari SE	19	3680	480	4500	17 3/4"
2008	Safari SE	20	3965	600	5000	17 3/4"
2008	Safari SE FB	23	4460	600	6000	17 3/4"
2008	Safari SE	23	4757	500	6000	
2008	Safari SE	25	5065	860	7000	17 3/4"
2008	Safari SE SS	25	5380	750	7300	17 3/4"
2008	Safari SE FB	25	5210	720	7300	17 3/4"
2008	Safari SE	27	5399	790	7600	17 3/4"
2008	Safari SE	28	5495	830	7300	17 3/4"
2008	International DWR	16	3080	480	4300	17 3/4"
2008	International Signature Series	16	2825	430	3500	18"
2008	International Signature Series	19	3575	510	4500	17 1/4"
2008	International Signature Series	23	4695	700	6000	17 3/4"
2008	International Signature Series SS	25	5145	740	7000	17 3/4"
2008	International Signature Series FB	25	5410	820	7300	17 3/4"
2008	International Signature Series	27	5813	790	7600	17 3/4"
2008	International Signature Series	28	5440	880	7300	17 3/4"
2008	International Ocean Breeze	16	2825	430	3500	18"
2008	International Ocean Breeze	19	3575	510	4500	17 1/4"
2008	International Ocean Breeze	23	4695	700	6000	17 3/4"
2008	International Ocean Breeze	25	5145	740	7000	17 3/4"
2008	International Ocean Breeze	25	5410	820	7300	17 3/4"

Year	Name	Length	Dry Wt.	Hitch Wt.	GVWR	Hitch Ball Height
2008	International Ocean Breeze	27	5813	790	7600	17 3/4"
2008	International Ocean Breeze	28	5440	880	7300	17 3/4"
2008	Classic	25	5900	780	8000	18 3/4"
2008	Classic	27	6525	790	9000	18 3/4"
2008	Classic	30	7095	670	10000	18 3/4"
2008	Classic FB	30	6883	860	10000	
2008	Classic S/O	30	7940	1050	10300	19 3/4"
2008	Classic	31	7050	760	10000	18 3/4"
2008	Classic	34	7858	770	11500	18 3/4"
2008	Classic S/O	34	8247	1150	11500	19 3/4"
2008	BaseCamp	16	1965	350	3250	18"
2008	Interstate	22	8436	N/A	11030	N/A
2009	Interstate	22	8436	N/A	11030	N/A
2009	Interstate Twin	22	7976	N/A	11030	N/A
2009	PanAmerica	34	7225	1260	11500	19 3/4"
2009	Sport	17	2800	300	3500	16 1/2"
2009	Sport	22	3350	370	4000	17 1/4"
2009	Flying Cloud	19	3680	480	4500	17 3/4"
2009	Flying Cloud	20	3965	600	5000	17 3/4"
2009	Flying Cloud	23	4460	600	6000	17 3/4"
2009	Flying Cloud FB	23	4757	500	6250	17 3/4"
2009	Flying Cloud	25	5210	720	7300	17 3/4"
2009	Flying Cloud	27	5399	790	7600	17 3/4"
2009	Flying Cloud	28	5495	830	7300	17 3/4"
2009	International DWR	16	3080	480	4300	18"
2009	International Signature Series	16	2825	430	3500	18"
2009	International Signature Series	19	3575	510	4500	17 1/4"
2009	International Signature Series	23	4695	700	6000	17 3/4"
2009	International Signature Series SS	25	5145	740	7000	17 3/4"
2009	International Signature Series FB	25	5410	820	7300	17 3/4"
2009	International Signature Series	27	5813	790	7600	17 3/4"
2009	International Signature Series	28	5440	880	7300	17 3/4"
2009	International Ocean Breeze	16	2825	430	3500	18"
2009	International Ocean Breeze	19	3575	510	4500	17 1/4"
2009	International Ocean Breeze	23	4695	700	6000	17 3/4"

Year	Name	Length	Dry Wt.	Hitch Wt.	GVWR	Hitch Ball Height
2009	International Ocean Breeze SS	25	5145	740	7000	17 3/4"
2009	International Ocean Breeze FB	25	5410	820	7300	17 3/4"
2009	International Ocean Breeze	27	5813	790	7600	17 3/4"
2009	International Ocean Breeze	28	5440	880	7300	17 3/4"
2009	Classic	25	5900	780	8000	18 3/4"
2009	Classic	27	6525	790	9000	18 3/4"
2009	Classic	30	7095	670	10000	18 3/4"
2009	Classic FB	30	6883	860	10000	18 3/4"
2009	Classic S/O	30	7940	1050	10300	19 3/4"
2009	Classic	31	7050	760	10000	18 3/4"
2009	Classic	34	7858	770	11500	18 3/4"
2009	Classic S/O	34	8247	1150	11500	19 3/4"
2010	INTL BAMBI	16	2,825	430	4,300	
2010	INTL BAMBI CSA	16	2,825	430	4,300	
2010	INTL BAMBI	19	3,575	510	4,500	
2010	INTL BAMBI CSA	19	3,575	510	5,000	
2010	INTL	23D	4,695	700	6,000	
2010	INTL CSA	23D	4,695	700	6,300	
2010	INTL	25FB	5,410	820	7,300	
2010	INTL	27FB	5,813	790	7,600	
2010	INTL	28	5,440	880	7,300	
2010	FLYING CLOUD - CSA	19	3,725	570	5,000	
2010	FLYING CLOUD	20	4,197	640	5,000	
2010	FLYING CLOUD	23	4,707	730	6,000	
2010	FLYING CLOUD - CSA	23	4,707	730	6,300	
2010	FLYING CLOUD	23	4,757	500	6,000	
2010	FLYING CLOUD - CSA	23	4,757	500	6,300	
2010	FLYING CLOUD	25	5,477	760	7,300	
2010	FLYING CLOUD	27	5,600	775	7,600	
2010	FLYING CLOUD	28	5,700	950	7,300	
2010	VICTORINOX	19	3,800	583	4,500	
2010	SPORT	16	2,800	300	3,500	
2010	SPORT	17	3,043	300	3,500	
2010	SPORT CSA	17	3,043	300	4,500	
2010	SPORT	22	3,515	367	4,500	

Year	Name	Length	Dry Wt.	Hitch Wt.	GVWR	Hitch Ball Height
2010	CLASSIC	27 FB	6,525	790	9,000	
2010	CLASSIC	30	7,095	670	10,000	
2010	CLASSIC W/DINETTE	31	7,050	760	10,000	
2010	PAN AMERICA	34	7,480	1,490	11,500	
	AEU TRAILERS					
2010	422 SPORT	422			2910	
2010	532 INTERNATIONAL 2.3	532	3020	187/220	3748	
2010	534 INTERNATIONAL 2.3	534	3020	187/220	3748	
2010	684 INTERNATIONAL 2.3	684	3880	243/330	4828	
2010	534 INTERNATIONAL 2.5	534	3086	187/220	3968	
2010	684 INTERNATIONAL 2.5	684	4000	243/330	5049	
2010	NCV3		8,514		11,030	
2010	NCV3 Twin		8,213		11,030	

The Vintage Airstream Podcast

The Vintage Airstream Podcast show archive
available at www.theVAP.com

PERFECT POLISH

Materials and Techniques for a Mirror- Like Finish

Polishing for Perfectionists

Visit us at:
www.PefectPolish.com
or call us at:
(877)370-0269

Cyclo
Polishers

Nuvite Aluminum
Polish

Compounding
Polishers

Cyclo Polishing
Kits

Polishing Cloth

Compounding
Polishing Kits

Visit us at PerfectPolish.com

Subscribe to the podcast for free at www.theVAP.com

34260904R00167

Made in the USA
Middletown, DE
14 August 2016